TEAM TEACHING

Bold New Venture

TEAM TEACHING

Bold New Venture

Edited by

DAVID W. BEGGS, III

Introduction by

HAROLD SPEARS

INDIANA UNIVERSITY PRESS

BLOOMINGTON & LONDON

To
J. LLOYD TRUMP,
a man of vision who asked American
educators to evaluate, to think and
to act.

SIXTH PRINTING 1969

Copyright © 1964 by Indiana University Press
Library of Congress catalog card number: 64-17456
All Rights Reserved
Manufactured in the United States of America

253-35820-5

Bold New Venture Series
Preface

AMERICAN EDUCATION is emerging as a new frontier. Staggering challenges brought about by the contemporary demand for quality education for a bulging and diverse student population must be met. Old solutions for new problems will not suffice.

Pioneer educators are testing promising new programs and practices to effect fundamental improvement in the schools. Healthy dissatisfactions have led to the belief that if the schools are to be significantly better, they will have to be substantially different. Both the substance and the form of instruction are undergoing searching reappraisal. Exciting innovations have been instituted in schools scattered throughout the country. The *Bold New Venture* series is designed to inform educators and the interested public about these new developments and to assist in their evaluation.

The books in this series differ from much of the professional literature in education. The contributors, for the most part, are practitioners. Admittedly they are partial to their topics. Nevertheless, pitfalls are exposed and candid treatment is given to the issues. Emphasis has been put on reporting *how* as well as *why* new practices and programs were inaugurated. The volumes in this series are intended to be a stimulus to the conversation which must take place if fresh methods of teaching are to find their way into the schools.

Topics included in the *Bold New Venture* series include team teaching, flexible scheduling, independent study, the nongraded school, instructional materials centers, data processing, small group instruction, and technological aids.

While journalists criticize, scholars theorize about, and philosophers analyze education, the teachers of America must act. Educators must leap from theory to practice in individualizing instruction. More responsibility must be given and accepted by youngsters for their own learning. Intellectual inquiry must become full-time, leisure-time, and life-time pursuits.

Progress in education does not always come by the process of addition with more teachers, more books, more courses, and more money. Real improvement can come from original uses of scarce human talent, precious time, and new methods.

Because it is intended primarily for teachers and administrators, the *Bold New Venture* series focuses on the practical problems of teaching. What has been operationally successful for some teachers may have application for other teachers. If new practices or programs result from these books, then the series will have fulfilled its aim, for the *Bold New Venture* books are calls and guides to action.

D.W.B.
E.G.B.

Bloomington, Indiana

Contents

Introduction

IT IS AN HONOR to introduce a book that is worthy of the attention of those seeking better ways of organizing their schools for instructional effectiveness. It has always been exciting to me to examine these promising road maps to the hidden treasures of our profession—road maps that appear too infrequently.

There has been the extra thrill of seeing a book in its preliminary stage, of reading the galley proofs before they were cut into pages and sewn between covers. Those who have written this book might be termed miners who have been prospecting out in the fields of team teaching. Their enthusiastic accounts are stimulating and encouraging to the uninformed.

Within a period of a very few years, team teaching has taken such a hold upon the imagination of the curriculum-conscious that a school practitioner finds himself at a loss in an instructional gathering unless he is familiar with its ideas and the current experience in its application. Here is a book to raise his team teaching quotient. However, as the authors cautiously point out, whether team teaching is to be adopted in a local school system depends upon numerous factors, factors which are well defined. In teaching there are no panaceas, merely proven practices and promising ideas, both of which call for realism and hard work.

I was invited to introduce this book because of my own extensive experience with one of the forerunners of team teaching, namely the core curriculum.* An innovation of the late thirties and the early forties, many of its principles and early patterns are bobbing up again in team teaching.

Among the common features are (1) a large group of pupils assigned to a team of teachers, (2) a curriculum block assigned as the area to be covered, (3) a block of time longer than the usual period

---

* Editor's note: Dr. Spears's own book on the core curriculum is *The Emerging High School Curriculum,* published in 1940 by the American Book Company.

provided for the work, (4) the provision within the program of class groups varying in size from exceedingly large to exceedingly small, (5) freedom for the teachers to plan among themselves the flexible scheduling within the program that meets the instructional objectives of the moment and (6) the correlation of curriculum content naturally related.

The concept of team teaching is much more matured and has broader application than the earlier core program, as is readily apparent in this new book.

Following are some of the lessons in the earlier experience which must be faced realistically in securing the benefits of the team teaching movement:

1. Any group of teachers, given the right to carry on a flexible team program, may in time standardize their organizational procedures to the extent that they have established, without realizing it, another fixed pattern as static as the one against which they rebelled. Security can easily overcome flexibility.

2. Any extreme change in curriculum pattern calls for an administrative leader who has no doubts about the undertaking. He must become just as much a student of the enterprise as the teachers who team together. Any curriculum experiment calls for administrative protection against the doubting Thomas, be he professional or layman.

3. The teacher who pools his lot with others in a cooperative program, in contrast to his right to plan alone and teach alone, must be an enthusiastic participant rather than a reluctant draftee. The administration must always be ready with a replacement in the wings.

This book will be inviting to the large school that wants to break the lockstep of mass production, but likewise to the small school that wants to take greater instructional advantage of the more personal relationships that already exist due to the school's size.

A firm tie joins the past and the present of American education, and this accounts for the continuous progress that we make. In our search for the emerging school, we come to realize that we will never find it. Perhaps we never should. It is rather the spirit and the key to the great success of American education that we find.

The greatness of our nation exists not so much in possessing as in striving and searching for. There isn't the one best school or the one right idea. Team teaching, for instance, will not be exactly the same thing in any two schools.

The school exists partly in practice, partly in the minds of devoted teachers and administrators and conscientious citizens. That is its salvation. Excellence results from the kind of stimulation of thought and effort that comes when we are seeking a better classroom than we had the year before. And that is the kind of stimulation you will find between these covers.

Happy reading!

HAROLD SPEARS

San Francisco, California   *Superintendent of Schools*

TEAM TEACHING

Bold New Venture

CHAPTER 1

What Team Teaching Really Is

by

IRA J. SINGER

Currently Director of Curriculum Research for the Board of Cooperative Educational Services, Erie County, New York, Dr. Ira J. Singer is one of the country's most noted consultants on team teaching and other staff utilization projects.

He holds three degrees from New York University, an A.B., M.A. and a doctorate in education, and served for several years as a staff associate for the Committee on Staff Utilization, National Association of Secondary School Principals.

Dr. Singer is well known as a speaker and lecturer. In addition, he has helped set up team teaching programs in various school systems throughout the eastern United States.

TEAM TEACHING is an exciting concept.

It is an organizational device which encompasses all aspects of the teaching-learning experience. Properly planned and executed, the team pattern invites a searching reappraisal of such factors as educational objectives, teacher role, school schedule, class size, curriculum development, staff morale, facilities design, staffing patterns, teacher-teacher, student-student, student-teacher and teacher-student relationships, school-community relations, salary structure and accreditation procedures.

The all-embracing nature of the team concept can make anyone uneasy about considering conversion from present practices to team teaching. He may question the necessity for change before he bothers to investigate the new plan. After all, why waste time on new practices if present methods are educationally sound?

13

Present Practices—A Short Quiz

To avoid the risk of a voluminous analysis of contemporary education, some pointed questions reflective of typical conditions under which teachers labor in most American schools are here offered. These questions were gathered from hundreds of teachers interviewed by the writer while he served as staff associate for the Committee on Staff Utilization. The reader is urged to consider himself a classroom teacher and silently respond to the following:

• Do you feel that you are successful in identifying, diagnosing and treating individual differences of youngsters when you teach 150 students per day, five days per week?

• Have you ever dared hope for the day when, as part of the schedule, you could sit with twelve or fifteen students, informally guiding a discussion and acting as a resource person?

• Did you ever want to send certain students to the laboratory, shop or music room, as well as to the library for independent study, only to discover that it just isn't done, or there is no supervision, or the schedule won't allow it? In the same vein, did you ever captain a study hall and murmur, "There must be a better way?"

• Have you ever felt particularly exhilarated about one or several areas of the curriculum in which you are particularly knowledgeable and effective? Did you ever conceitedly think that, with your special background knowledge of the cultures of Latin America or the reconstruction period, you could effectively motivate three or four classes at one time?

• Have you ever wished for a work place of your own, away from your desk, where you could create materials, preview visuals and recordings, read current literature in your field, evaluate student materials or just escape from the isolation of the classroom to meet professionally with your colleagues?

• Have you ever had a secret desire to watch someone else teach without being concerned about others thinking you insecure; or have you wanted another teacher to watch you without fearing that others would think you a showoff?

• Have you ever felt that you wasted precious time as you patrolled corridors, monitored yards and cafeterias, sold tickets to school games, policed crowds at these games, mimeographed tests, graded objective tests, spent hours at registration forms, proctored study halls and kept house?

• Have you ever felt despair in your classes where, despite your devices, discussions are dominated by the same students each day?

• Have you ever felt embarrassed or a bit sad upon returning tests a week or more after they have been submitted?

• Have you ever wished that you could ring the bell yourself to make the period longer for certain lessons and shorter for others, or have you ever wished to short-circuit the bell system completely?

• Have you ever looked with jaundiced eye on a student teacher trying to cram the applied aspects of teaching into a few short months?

• Have you ever wanted to rearrange your room or divide it into several areas or individual cubicles? Have you been prevented from doing this by the permanence of certain walls and fixtures?

If you answered "Yes, but . . ." to 90 per cent or more of these questions, then you suffer the same frustrations as do the majority of your teaching colleagues. If you answered "No!" to all or most of these questions, then you would be well advised to write your own book rather than read this one.

Birth and Background of Team Teaching

A glimpse of the motives underlying team teaching is now possible. The continuing curriculum explosion, the population boom and the acute shortage of teaching personnel inspired the establishment of the Commission on Curriculum Planning and Development by the National Association of Secondary School Principals in 1956. This group, dedicated to the spirit of innovation, decided to launch a series of experimental projects in secondary schools throughout the country. These projects were designed to devise new approaches to the critical problems confronting the schools: curriculum development, teaching methods and space and staff utilization.

After soliciting and receiving hundreds of ideas and research designs from schools across the nation, the Commission, under the leadership of J. Lloyd Trump, submitted to the Fund for the Advancement of Education *A Proposal Designed to Demonstrate How Improved Teacher-Utilization Can Help to Solve the Problem of Teacher Shortage in the High Schools of the United States*. The Fund approved the proposal and agreed to provide financial support to schools, selected by the Commission, to develop various staff utilization techniques. Perhaps the most significant of these techniques became known as team teaching.

In more than 100 schools throughout the country, serious investigations of the team approach to instruction were launched. The most complete accounts of these experiments have appeared in *The Bulletin of the National Association of Secondary School Principals.* Other popular sources for learning the theory and practice underlying the Commission projects have been the Committee on Staff Utilization, a consultative group organized to disseminate the findings of the staff utilization experiments; the film "And No Bells Ring"; a series of booklets by Trump; and the film strip "Focus on Change." Major impetus to the progress of team teaching also was provided by Harvard University and Claremont College of California.

Team Teaching—Theme and Variations

THEME

Despite the many interpretations of the phrase "team teaching," and the numerous acts committted under its name, a basic definition is possible—though it is as flexible as the practice itself.

Team teaching may be defined as *an arrangement whereby two or more teachers, with or without teacher aides, cooperatively plan, instruct and evaluate one or more class groups in an appropriate instructional space and given length of time, so as to take advantage of the special competencies of the team members.*

Though this broad definition does not begin to tell the tale of the many variations of team teaching, it does suggest several major factors basic to any team plan:

cooperative planning, instruction and evaluation

student grouping for special purposes (large group instruction, small group discussion, independent study)

flexible daily schedule

use of teacher aides

recognition and utilization of individual teacher talents

use of space and media appropriate to the purpose and content of instruction.

VARIATIONS

Although few plans are exactly alike, three patterns are emerging from activity across the country. These patterns might be termed the single-discipline team, the interdisciplinary team and the school-within-school team.

* These descriptions may be found in the January issues, 1958-1962, and in the May, 1963, issue.

Single-discipline team. The single-discipline team usually consists of two or three teachers from the same department, teaming together to instruct a common set of students. Teaching periods may be scheduled side by side or consecutively.

For example, the teachers of two tenth-grade social studies classes may team during the first period of each day so that each teacher can instruct that phase of the course which he can best handle. This arrangement exposes a teacher's specific talents to twice as many students as in the conventional schedule (Figs. 1 and 2). Such a team may be organized to permit a new teacher to work with a veteran teacher, providing a built-in-service program. With an instructional assistant, a clerical aide and additional planning time, the team members can practice continuous curriculum planning and revision based on the needs of their students as well as their own assets and abilities. To further the activities of this team, community resource specialists, outstanding films, self-instruction programs and other essential technological learning tools can be brought into the pattern.

TIME	MONDAY	TUESDAY	WEDNESDAY	THURSDAY	FRIDAY
8:00- 8:50	Hist. 10A	Hist. 10A	Hist. 10A	Hist. 10A	Hist. 10A
	Hist. 10B	Hist. 10B	Hist. 10B	Hist. 10B	Hist. 10B

FIG. 1.—CONVENTIONAL SCHEDULE

TIME	MONDAY	TUESDAY	WEDNESDAY	THURSDAY	FRIDAY
8:00- 8:50	History 10AB (LG)	History 10AB1* (SG) History 10AB2 (SG) History 10AB3 (SG)	History 10AB (LG)	History 10AB1* (SG) History 10AB2 (SG) History 10AB3 (SG)	History 10AB (IS) Project work in library, laboratory, music room, art studio, etc.

(60 students, 2 teachers, 1 instruction assistant)
* One History 10AB-SG can be supervised by an instruction assistant, student teacher or student leader. LG = large group, SG = small group, IS = independent study.

FIG. 2.—SINGLE-DISCIPLINE TEAM SCHEDULE

Although this type of team is most often restricted to a single forty-five or fifty-minute period, alternate possibilities do exist for providing large group–small group–independent study instruction during the fixed period. For example, one team member of a three-teacher team can present large group instruction to sixty students of a ninety-student group. While he lectures to the sixty, the remaining thirty may be broken into two groups of fifteen. Each group is then assigned to another team teacher or instructional assistant. The students may then be rotated through the special size groupings according to a formula set by the team (Fig. 3). Although this is not the most desirable system, it does afford some flexibility when team activities are restricted to the fixed daily period.

TIME	MONDAY	TUESDAY	WEDNESDAY	THURSDAY	FRIDAY
	Group A1, A2, A3 LG-60 students	Group B&C LG-30 students	Group A1, A2 LG-40 students	Group A3, B, C LG-50 students	Group A1 SG-20 students
	Group B SG-15 students	Group A IS-20 students	Group A3 IS-20 students	Group A1 SG-20 students	Group A3 SG-20 students
8:00-8:50	Group C SG-15 students	Group A2 SG-20 students	Group B SG-15 students	Group A2 SG-20 students	Group B IS-15 students
		Group A3 SG-20 students	Group C SG-15 students		Group C IS-15 students
					Group A2 IS-20 students

(90 students, 3 teachers, 1 instructional assistant)

FIG. 3.—FLEXIBILITY FOR SINGLE-DISCIPLINE WITHIN
A DAILY ONE-PERIOD SCHEDULE.

Occasionally, the single-discipline team may be organized on a block-of-time schedule. However, this arrangement is usually reserved for the interdisciplinary or school-within-school team.

The popularity of the single-discipline team has been due primarily to the ease with which it can be employed within a conventional schedule. Administrators and teachers have not found it too upsetting to combine classes into large groups or break them into smaller groups so long as the master schedule is not radically retooled. In Pittsford,

New York, the schedule was revised so that each of the large group classes met twice weekly for double periods of ninety minutes. The large groups were then divided into seminar sections of eight to fourteen students meeting once a week. Seminar sections were ability-grouped with terminal students, excluded from the project, meeting in conventional classes.

In West Irondequoit, New York, a team of five teachers in eleventh-grade English (American literature) share the large group and small group work equally. A teacher conducts two large group lectures (one a repeat), fifteen small group seminar and five conventional classes each week. In addition, he has a double period each day for planning team activities.

Interdisciplinary Block of Time Team. The interdisciplinary block of time team consists of teachers from different disciplines given a common block of time to use as the team sees fit for the instruction of a common set of students in classes of flexible size.

For example, an administrator may assign a two-period block of time to a social studies/English team; a three-period block of time to a social studies/English/science team, etc. Once the block is assigned, the team assumes the major responsibility for scheduling large group, small group and independent study activities within the block (Fig. 4).

TIME	MONDAY	TUESDAY	WEDNESDAY	THURSDAY	FRIDAY
8:00 9:00	Two English teachers team with 2 history teachers to teach 120 students for a 120-minute block of time scheduled as the team desires for LG, SG, IS situations.				
10:00	Team Planning				

(120 students, 4 teachers, 1 aide)
FIG. 4.—INTERDISCIPLINARY BLOCK OF TIME TEAM

This type of schedule permits the teacher to reduce such undesirable practices as padding or cutting lessons in order to meet a static bell schedule. In the illustration, the 120-minute block may be treated as a weekly or daily figure. The team may prefer to schedule a weekly 600-minute block (120 × 5) rather than the daily 120-minute block. They may set certain goals for the week and assign chunks of time for large group, small group and independent study. They may look at the block as a monthly interval and devote entire weeks to one type of activity or another. Whether daily, weekly or monthly, the team can divide the block into modules of fifteen or twenty minutes and fit the various large group, small group and independent study activities into multiples of these modules.

In Racine, Wisconsin, the junior high school established a team teaching system under an English-social studies block organization. Students attended double periods of English and social studies in three sections during the same period in the morning and again in the afternoon. A seventh-grade team of three teachers handled the morning and afternoon blocks of ninety students per block. They then planned the curriculum, schedule, teacher assignment and evaluation procedure cooperatively. The team also utilized a team leader and an instructional secretary serving both morning and afternoon teams.

At Upland High School in Upland, California, the team project operates within the regular school schedule, with all team classes meeting during the first four periods in the morning. However, the team teachers are free to use modules of time in accordance with their instructional needs, shifting from regular academic class sessions to large group instruction. They may team in pairs or assume tutorial roles for independent study. They may group their classes to be tested, group-counseled or for community resource specialist lectures, or they may shift back to small units for individual counseling. All team teachers meet for planning purposes during the fifth period.

School-Within-School Team. The school-within-school team consists of teachers from all disciplines, responsible for the instruction of the same body of students over an extended period of time, usually two to four years. Flexibility in class size and schedule is maintained in this pattern.

The primary purpose of this type of team is to encourage a closer relationship between teacher and student within any and all disciplines. In a large school, the loss of identity suffered by some students might be compensated by placing them in a smaller "division" of the larger school. This "division" may be called a house plan, a form, a school or some similar name. By using the shifting patterns of the team arrangement, teachers observe the behavior and performance of their students in various learning situations during this extended period of time. In the small school, this kind of team attempts to approach the problem of treating individual differences of students in a realistic and continuous manner. Such teams have encouraged members of the various "division" faculties to exchange assignments and have permitted students to take instruction in other "divisions" from time to time in order to introduce greater variety into the pattern.

The Claremont Graduate School in Claremont, California, has sponsored experimentation with the small, integrated school-within-school teaching team. The teams participating in this project usually consist of a group of five to six teachers given a small body of about 150 students for a period of time longer than one or two semesters. Students attend classes of shifting size and schedule (usually block or modular). Teacher strengths are magnified by schedules compiled by the team under the direction of a team leader. Team members are given three to five periods per week to meet for team planning conferences during the school day. The counseling and guidance functions are integral parts of the team operation.

Hierarchical Considerations. Within these three basic types of teaching teams, certain hierarchical differences may be noted. In San Diego, California, groups of 100 met for large group instruction under the experienced teacher in charge; for small group discussions under a certificated teacher (with less experience) and assistant teachers, all of whom were helped by clerk-aides who handled the clerical chores. A number of the assistant teachers were student trainees from the San Diego State Teachers College on a five-year training program.

In Melbourne, Florida, a group of eighty-four students was given algebra instruction by a team consisting of a master teacher, assistant teacher, general aide and student aide. The first two were full-time, qualified mathematics teachers sharing the large group and independent tutoring responsibilities. Small group discussion occurred in groups of seven students conducted by a workshop-trained student leader. The general aide performed the paper grading, recording, mimeographing and other clerical duties. This arrangement worked particularly well in the non-graded, phased education program at Melbourne High School.

In Evanston, Illinois, as part of the English 3 Project, a team of seven teachers divided the work load as follows:

1. Three teachers were responsible for the large group instruction and three of the small class sections.

2. One teacher was responsible for large group instruction and two small class sections.

3. One teacher was responsible for two small class sections.

4. Two teachers were each responsible for one small class section.

Special attention was paid to combining beginning teachers with veterans and to capitalizing on special teacher talents in working with large or small groups. In addition to the teaching staff, one part-time secretary-clerk took attendance in the large group room, mimeographed materials and gave make-up tests. An art consultant prepared visual materials.

Danger of Fragmentation

Caution should be taken in accepting these thumbnail descriptions of team patterns as yardsticks of quality and design for all existing teams. Many teams have departed from these team patterns and hierarchical organizations. A recent survey for the N.A.S.S.P. turned up the interesting fact that in six states, 517 schools professed "occasional team teaching" while 129 schools affirmed a "systematic" team organization. With several notable exceptions, the projects were not generally characterized by daring or boldness.

Team teaching still suffers from fragmentation and is not yet the synthesis of learning experiences it was meant to be. The N.A.S.S.P. survey scores the woeful inactivity and conservatism in changing lockstep time patterns and obsolete facilities. Despite a reported increase in team teaching activity, few schools indicated a willingness to make simultaneous changes in student grouping, class size and daily schedule.

SCHEDULE MODIFICATION

Unrealistic evaluation may also result from attempts on the part of some schools to treat individual needs through team teaching without schedule modification. Such modification may range from a moderate change, to permit team members to enjoy a daily common planning period, to a more extreme approach which at Brookhurst Junior High School, Anaheim, California, sees the complete schedule for the entire ninth grade changed every three days; or at Melbourne High School, Melbourne, Florida, where non-graded classes are taught by teaching teams in a phased (ability level) structure for each discipline; or at Lakeview High School, Decatur, Illinois, where a modular schedule permits all students to walk about the building according to the demands of their instructional needs rather than those of an unyielding master schedule. Schedule flexibility, then, is an integral feature of a comprehensive team teaching program and should be prerequisite to a realistic, over-all team teaching evaluation.

Possible Effects on Staff

Staff morale may also be tested during an evaluation period. Referring to the Harvard University evaluation of the Newton Plan experiment, Harold Howe commented:

> Those of us involved in a new project made emotional commitments to it. Then when the researchers with statistical viewpoints came out and started to pin us down, they rapidly ran into our emotions. This frustrated them and annoyed us. . . .
> At this point, the Newton-Harvard relationship is established on a firm basis as a result of having been through the fire together. While we were there, it wasn't particularly comfortable. *

As partners on a teaching team, teachers must learn to cultivate self-criticism and accept criticism, whether it be constructive or destructive, from colleagues. An elementary school principal in Texas told of placing two very good friends on the same elementary school team. After two weeks these friends were quarreling and at the close of the semester had to be placed in different schools. As Heller writes:

> Perhaps in no other teaching situation is the need for initial understanding among the faculty members as important and vital to the success of an enterprise. It is not easy for teachers to share their ideas in a manner which is free from excessive ego involvement, professional jealousies and biases.†

TEACHER ASSIGNMENTS

There is the persistent question of whether or not to "freeze" teachers into specific roles as large group instructors or small group leaders. Teachers who excel with large groups can profit from working with small groups from time to time so that an exchange of views can be conducted on a more intimate basis. However, this practice should be approached with some caution.

Although it is a good idea for each member of the team to participate in all phases of instruction, no attempt should be made to subor-

---

* Newtonville Public Schools, "The Principal Answered Some Questions," Newtonville, Mass., 1959 (mimeographed).

† Heller, Melvin P., and Belford, Elizabeth, "Team Teaching and Staff Utilization in Ridgewood High School," *The Bulletin*, January, 1962, p. 105.

dinate a specific talent to a time regimen which for purposes of convenience highlights weakness and de-emphasizes strength.

TEAM LEADER

Team teaching schools have indicated strong support for some type of team chairman, leader, coordinator, etc., to assume responsibility for the collective planning of the diverse activities of the team, for training teacher aides, contacting community resource specialists and coordinating team activities with the program of the rest of the school. However, some schools prefer to avoid the appointment of a designated team leader in order to avoid new salary and status implications.

Actually, the position of team leader is popular but additional compensation is rare. In some cases, team leaders do nothing to justify their positions. Some become dictators while others are appointed to relieve the administrator of certain duties unrelated to team planning. Clearly, the inference is that a team leader can be extremely helpful provided he fulfills a role specifically designed to plan, coordinate and direct the team program.

TEACHER AIDES

If a team teaching model is to be validly constructed, team members must be encouraged and permitted to expend *all* their energies in the planning and execution of instruction. This suggests that such non-teaching tasks as monitoring corridors and cafeterias, taking attendance, proctoring study halls, mimeographing papers, grading objective exams, reading themes for mechanical errors and other non-teaching tasks be assumed by auxiliary personnel.

The Bay City Teacher Aide Project in 1955 served to dramatize the need for such auxiliary personnel to help combat the growing teacher shortage. Although the shortage in most subject areas remains acute, teacher aides have played a prominent role in making this condition less painful. These aides have been particularly helpful on teaching teams. The assistance provided by student teachers working as team aides enables teams to cover more subject matter in greater depth than conventional classes without such additional assistance.

The following types of aides were reported to the N.A.S.S.P. survey:

student teachers from teacher training programs
college students (non-teacher trainees)
clerical workers

college-trained adults from the community

other adults (not college-trained)

The primary functions of these aides were reported as:

laboratory supervisors

lay readers of some written work

objective test graders

teachers for make-up or remedial work by individuals or small
   groups

hall or playground supervisors

study hall supervisors

library assistants

shop supervisors

clerical workers

Although the teacher aide has not solved the teacher shortage, his value appears high for teaching teams, where as an integral part of a system of instruction, he can release qualified teachers from non-teaching tasks for the more demanding jobs of preparing and executing instruction.

Assumptions for Progress

Assumptions for team teaching stated by Trump in 1957 are truer than ever today. In *New Horizons for Secondary School Teachers,* he wrote:

1. The quality of education depends largely on the quality of teaching.

2. The results of instruction depend largely on the ways in which teachers function in a school.

3. Methods of teaching should be related to the purposes of instruction.

4. Different levels of competence and training are needed for the various functions teachers now perform and which they are likely to do in the future.

5. Teachers differ in their interests and abilities to perform the various functions of teaching.

To these the writer would add:

6. Schools must continually meet new educational needs created by changes in our society.

7. The results of experimental research must be communicated intelligibly and rapidly to the classroom teacher in order to improve instructional programs.

These assumptions are basic to any team teaching plan contemplated by the educational community. However, in accepting the assumptions, one should recognize the limitations as well as the opportunities of team teaching.

Limitations of Team Teaching

ECONOMY

Team teaching is not a magic formula for saving money.

Efforts to embark on a team project as an excuse to create large classes, decrease professional services and increase the existing work load are doomed to failure. Such purposes may result in the saving of a few dollars but will have disastrous effects on student learning, school curricula and staff attitudes.

Economy may be accomplished by creating a wealth of visuals and other instructional materials as a permanent school resource, by using teacher aides for non-teaching tasks at salaries lower than teachers are currently paid for performing those same tasks and by the design of instructional spaces flexible enough to avoid early obsolescence, costly additions and renovations.

For the school completely geared to a conventional program, the initial costs of conversion to team teaching can range from moderate to high depending on the school's commitment. The costs of overhead and slide projectors, altered spaces, such special team aides as graphic arts technicians and lay readers, a training workshop for prospective team teachers, new and higher-salaried positions—all suggest additional expenditure of funds.

However, experience shows that, as the team project matures, the major concern becomes the reapportionment of funds to buy a better instructional program rather than perpetual support of an inferior brand of education.

EFFECTS ON CURRICULUM

Introducing team teaching will not change the curriculum overnight.

However, the organizational patterns of the team can create independent and group study situations more likely to enhance curriculum planning and revision than the fixed, isolated structures of the self-contained or departmentalized classrooms. The team must constantly examine and review the curriculum in its planning sessions.

The team structure also permits a natural cross-pollination of ideas for teachers trained in new curriculum projects, such as those sponsored by the National Science Foundation. Teachers working on the same team as representatives to such workshops can integrate much of the new material into their own teaching plans.

EFFECTS ON TIME

Teachers will not save time by participating in team teaching.

Instead, they will have more time to plan and teach than to monitor cafeterias and repeat lessons. In many schools, team teachers have had the additional responsibility of teaching conventional classes. Some feel that this is a good way to provide an informal basis of comparison for the teacher. However, the arrangement does suggest an additional preparation. To the time-starved team teacher involved in producing materials, writing outlines, delivering lectures, leading discussions, recruiting human resources, counseling independent learners and conferring with colleagues—additional classes of the conventional type are a detriment.

Summary of Objectives

Despite the limitations of the team method, the opportunities are rich and the potential vast. To summarize the objectives stated by team teaching schools throughout the country is to offer hope to the reader who sadly failed the quiz presented at the beginning of this chapter. Objectives of team teaching are directed at those areas of the instructional program either ignored or inadequately treated in the conventional school. These objectives might be stated as follows:

1. To develop creativity, adaptability, responsibility and habits of inquiry in students.

2. To make more intelligent use of teachers' specialized talents, interests, training, time and energy.

3. To improve the quality of teaching through the in-service nature of the team design.

4. To provide a program of student grouping which permits instruction to be more effectively geared to individual student ability.

5. To provide realistic *treatment* of individual differences to supplement the identifying and diagnosing of these differences.

6. To provide time and facilities during the school day for teachers

to prepare lessons, develop imaginative materials and keep abreast of new developments.

7. To provide students with group experiences prerequisite to successful citizenship in a democratic society.

To encourage people to meet these objectives is a difficult task. Some who strive to focus on the future are capable of seeing only a slightly altered image of the present; some are complacent; others lack courage; and some are just plain lazy. As Brickell points out in his report on innovation in the schools of New York State:

> Our greatest barrier in moving into a new plan will be our loyalty to the inadequate organizations and arrangements which exist today.
>
> If we can recognize them as being the best we could imagine when we invented them, give them full credit for what they *have* accomplished and then move on to something better, New York can maintain its long established leadership in education.*

For the most part, contributors to this volume have gone beyond present invention and found the going tough but exhilarating. As Archibald Shaw comments in *Overview*, "If there can be a single test of quality in an educational institution, it is a lovely dissatisfaction with things as they are and an active, open-minded search for ways to make them better."

In conducting such a search, courageous teachers and administrators are producing evidence to support the claim that any good instruction can be carried on in a team teaching setting.

* Brickell, Henry M., *Organizing New York for Educational Change* (Albany, N.Y., 1961).

CHAPTER 2

Fundamental Considerations
for Team Teaching

by

DAVID W. BEGGS, III

Formerly a high school principal and an assistant superin-
tendent of schools, David W. Beggs, III, now works with
the Senior High School of Indiana University's Laboratory
School at Bloomington, Indiana.

Mr. Beggs served as principal of Lakeview High School,
Decatur, Illinois, during the time the Decatur-Lakeview
Plan, a flexible scheduling-team teaching program, was
inaugurated. He has been a curriculum consultant for
some sixteen school districts for the past two years, and has
conducted workshops and institutes for teachers. In addi-
tion, he has written articles on team teaching for the pro-
fessional journals.

From his years of studying the question of how children
may best be taught, Mr. Beggs has come to feel that team
teaching—by its use of special talents—offers the answer.

BECAUSE team teaching is a theme with infinite variations, the term
"team teaching" is more descriptive than definitive. There are almost
as many differences between team teaching enterprises as there are
common characteristics shared. This is as it should be, for each school
needs to analyze its own instructional problems, set individual school
goals and shape its unique team approach.

The universal element in every team teaching formula is the cooperative focus on an instructional objective by more than one professional, with or without the supporting aid of non-certified technicians,
for a given group of students. The only defensible motive for team

teaching is the improvement, immediate or ultimate, of instruction. The universal key to successful team teaching lies in the most effective use of teaching talents and time.

Team teaching is both new and old. Cooperative endeavor within a teaching staff has been found frequently in good schools, but a planned program involving several teachers in a common instructional area is new.

The purpose here is to examine the basic elements of team teaching and to pinpoint the alternate possibilities in its application.

Varying circumstances in schools, situations with differing needs and differing professional resources make it unwise to suggest any universal approach to team teaching. But an assessment of the talents of a particular school's staff, in relation to that school's over-all objectives, will help identify the aspects of the total team teaching construct that should be exercised in a given situation. What makes sense for one school's program may be unrealistic in another school. The school's enrollment, the quality of its educational leadership and the rational use of human and material resources—all will influence the form of team teaching shaped for the school.

A realistic assessment, then, of a particular teaching staff's talents is the first step in organizing team teaching. At that point, too, it is important to raise basic questions on team mechanics, rather than to try and answer them during the actual planning stages of the team program, when more relevant questions will arise.

Some advocates of team teaching feel that its primary advantage lies in the increased quality of content transmitted to students. Others emphasize the organizational benefits that accrue to students after one teacher works with another on professional procedures and problems. The stimulation of team ideas and the evaluation of procedures used by more than one teacher can result in an improved quality of instruction for learners.

Decisions That Must Be Made

Before team teaching can succeed, the process of decision making in the school must be clearly identified by the leadership and accepted by the staff. That is, an individual (whether department head, principal, coordinator or superintendent) or group of individuals (curriculum committee, administrative council or board of education) must be able to sanction requests for varying the traditional approach to instruction. Because countless decisions need to be made for a team teaching program, the process by which these decisions are determined must be isolated and communicated to all members of the team. Without formal approval from a status person or group, any innovation, including team teaching, is doomed to unnecessary travail and ultimate failure.

Local school districts, varying in size, personnel competency and educational program, need to work out orderly decision making procedures to fit their own situations. The important factor is not which particular structure is developed to make decisions on team teaching, but that there be developed a recognized way of taking the best from the established method of teaching and using resources, and then adding the substance and quality of the team approach. All members of the school staff, whether a part of the teaching team or not, need to know both the method and the results of the decision making process. While most schools have defined the roles of the various members of the professional staff, many have not formalized the method by which changes can be officially made in the instructional materials and procedures used in the school.

Dimensions of Teaching Personnel

The heart of any instructional program, regardless of its organization, is the teaching staff. Countless conjectures have been made about the use of team teaching as a vehicle for improvement of staff competency. Research results have not substantiated this hypothesis, although it may have validity. If so, investigation is sorely needed to validate it.

What team teaching does, even if it may not improve teachers' skill, is to allow teachers to do for a large group those things they do best for a smaller group in a traditional class. That is, team teaching has the potential for extending good instruction to a greater area.

Team teaching gives teachers the advantage of working with other professionals in course planning, idea presentation, content reinforcement and program evaluation. Often a sense of loneliness prevails in a self-contained classroom when a teacher lacks stimulating contact with another teacher. Team teaching breaks down the walls of instructional isolation and invites the capabilities and efforts of several teachers to focus on common instructional problems.

In organizing a teaching team, care needs to be taken in considering the personal qualities of the various members. Team members must be people who work well with each other. A compatibility index can be structured and applied to the potential participants in any team teaching organization. In most schools this is done ultimately by the principal's subjective evaluation.

Professionals do not have to be personal friends to operate together effectively. Respect for competency and trust in motive are the most important attitudes for team members to have or to develop for each other.

Team teaching needs to be preceded by careful administrative planning of desired instructional or behavioral outcomes. Undefined expectations and goals nurture frustrations which would be avoided by candid communication between the teaching staff and the administrators before the team venture begins. Involvement in goal determination contributes to achievement by all the participants. Additionally, it is reasonable to invite the members of the teaching team to participate in determining the method by which the evaluation of team teaching will be made.

The composition of the teaching team can vary. It *may* be comprised only of certified members. There also may be teams with non-certified staff members (clerks or aides, people without a certificate to teach) playing a part in the cooperative instructional effort.

Chart 1

TEAM TEACHING PERSONNEL OPTIONS

A. Two or more full-time certified teachers.
B. Two or more full-time certified teachers and one or more non-certified aides.
C. Two or more full-time certified teachers assisted by a specialist as the need arises.

Some schools find advantage in using non-certified personnel, on either a full or part-time basis, to do clerical and other chores which do not involve contact with students. Some schools use resource specialists, who are not on the staff, as temporary members of the team. For instance, the city fire chief may work with the teaching team on a unit about fire prevention. When the unit is concluded, the resource specialist no longer is associated with the team.

Schools using only certified teachers on the team maintain there is little advantage in adding a clerical aide to the school's program. Their point is that all financial resources in a school should directly support additions to the professional staff. Funds earmarked for clerks obviously won't be reappropriated for additional teachers. On the other hand, those who advocate the use of non-certified aides insist there is an advantage to the teaching-learning process in the assistance clerks give directly to teachers and indirectly to students.

By handling these sub-professional chores, the aides (paraprofessionals) free teachers to work more with students as groups and as individuals.

Once the composition of the teaching team is determined, a decision needs to be made as to whether the team is to be a partnership of equals or composed of members with different responsibilities and status. Those who advocate the establishment of differentiated responsibility and status see this as a way to give supervision to new and inexperienced teachers, to recognize varying instructional competencies through role definition, to attach responsibility for group action to one person and to give honor and prestige to outstanding teachers. Various titles are given to team members. Some systems call the leader of the team chairman, master teacher, teacher presenter or teacher leader. Other certified teachers on the team are referred to as instructor, teacher specialist or teacher.

Chart 2

TEAM TEACHING ROLE ALTERNATIVES

A. Professional teachers with equal rank, status and responsibility.
B. Professional teachers with differentiated rank, status and responsibilities.
Non-certified workers may assist either of the teams.

On the other hand, those who prefer that teams be composed of professional equals argue that the team is more productive when the rank and status of all members is equal. Advocates of the team without differentiated rank contend that full interest and effort will go into the teaching enterprise by all the staff, while the graded organization might build up divisions, might allow some to abdicate responsibility and might create a barrier between fellow workers. Experience of other professionals tends to refute this argument. College educators find role differentiation helpful. Few legal offices or medical clinics are operated by professional equals, although they do not give titles—other than a name on the door—to the senior members of the organization.

It is important to determine at the outset whether or not the leadership role on the team is to be assigned or is to emerge. Clear communication of administrative decision on this issue is vital in giving a sense of security to the team members. If leadership is to be assigned, it must be based on an established set of criteria so it will be desired, not weakly accepted.

Some advocates of differentiating team member's roles see this as a way to a salary policy which compensates teachers at varying rates. Such advocates would have the determination of salary based on authority given and responsibility assumed. Educators who advocate different role responsibilities may go another step and provide extra compensation for superior quality within each role classification. For instance, all chairmen of teams would receive more compensation than other team members, while some chairmen might receive more money than others because of superior performance or extra effort. The interjection of the salary differential should not obscure the central reason for team teaching, the improvement of instruction. On the other hand, perhaps the salary differential practice may contribute to this goal over an extended period of time.

Some teachers are better at one aspect of instruction than at others. For example, one teacher may be able to bring students out in discussion and know how to listen for clues to depth of student understanding to a greater degree than another teacher. Such an instructor can give his talent to more students if he specializes in small group work. A second teacher may be best at expressing ideas in a clear and interesting way. Such a teacher usually employs some theatrical talent. This teacher often is more interested in content than individual student growth, while the small group teacher is characterized by concern for individuals and is somewhat less interested in content for its own sake. Together, the two teachers make an ideal team.

To ask a single teacher to be expert at content design, learning experience selection, presentation, discussion techniques and evaluation is a big order. Accordingly, there is merit in limiting the areas of instructional responsibilty so each teacher can become an expert in some phase of the team's operation. There are those teachers who have the skill, for example, to construct tests that teach as well as evaluate student progress. Such a teacher should do this for as many students as possible and not be restricted to a part of the student population.

It is human to gain satisfaction from doing the things one is good at doing. And when teachers are doing the things they like and are good at doing, a student can get the most benefit from the differing talents of several teachers. Students' learning groups can be organized in a variety of ways. The organization of a learning group within any course is bounded by:

1. content .... based on student needs and course goals
2. instructional procedures ..... determined by effective utilization of teachers' talent and content requirements
3. learning group size .... set by the nature of the learning activity
4. student composition .... based on common goals and a teachable range of achievement
5. duration of class meetings.... organized around the purpose of learning activity
6. frequency of class meetings.. established by requirements for mastery

CONTENT

The first criterion in organizing a learning group is content selection. Some teams will, as has been pointed out, work with content in one area and others will work with content in more than one area. Even within a content field and a grade level, teams frequently set up learning groups which explore content on different levels of complexity and depth, depending on the achievement level of the learners in the group. When the first team is established in a school, it is generally concerned with one content and one grade level. As team operation becomes more sophisticated, it tends to include interdisciplinary membership. For example, science teachers join the mathematics team.

INSTRUCTIONAL PROCEDURES

Once the basic content is determined for a team's discipline, it is necessary to identify the instructional procedures to be used. Sometimes lectures may be given; at other times discussions may be appropriate, or independent student work in the instructional materials center may be advisable. The teaching procedures determined as best in helping students to master content will dictate what the various members of the teaching team will need to do. Sometimes the team members will specialize in one role: lecturing, for example; on other teams the instructional work will be rotated on a regular or *ad hoc* basis. Teachers most dynamic at lecturing would handle this function. Others may work well with students in stimulating discussions or in developing effective work sheets.

A decision needs to be made as to whether team members will specialize in certain tasks or whether these various tasks will be rotated among all members of the team. A strong case can be made for specialization of function to develop real mastery of that function.

LEARNING GROUP SIZE

The learning group size should be determined by the nature of the learning activity. A study of the content will help the team members determine whether large groups, small groups or independent study time is needed. If the instructional procedure is to be a presentation by a teacher, it can be given to a large group (from 45 to 200 or more students) as efficiently and effectively as to a group of twenty-five. On the other hand, if the learning activity selected is discussion, then the class should contain no more than seven to fifteen students. Fruitful discussion can't go on in a class of thirty if there is to be a marked degree of individual student involvement. Thus, the class size can vary according to the team's determination of what instructional procedure will be appropriate.

Some schools have scheduled students into large groups and small groups on a regular basis for a semester or a year. Others have worked out the group size on a day-to-day basis. The judgment must be made as to whether a school wants to set a pattern for instruction and stick to it for an assigned time or whether reorganization of class groups should go on from day to day or week to week on an *ad hoc* basis.

STUDENT COMPOSITION

With few students in the small groups, an effective teacher can come close to individualizing instruction. Of course, a team may decide to keep the group size around the traditional number of twenty-five or thirty. But the composition and size of the various learning groups are matters for team determination. A school does not need to have a pattern of small and large group instruction to have team teaching. The potential for small and large group instruction becomes administratively possible, however, with team teaching.

DURATION OF CLASS MEETINGS

Class meeting lengths can be varied. A team may want half-hour lecture sessions and one or even two-hour discussion or laboratory classes. The duration of learning sessions is decided by the team according to the instructional procedures and the nature of the course content. Teachers of skill subjects often prefer fewer but longer weekly meetings than teachers of the traditional subjects. If the procedure to be used is discussion, then the class must be long enough to insure maximum student interaction. If the procedure is a lecture, then the class length should meet the extent of the students' attention span.

FREQUENCY OF CLASS MEETINGS

Classes do not need to meet every day of the week in all courses just as they do not have to be of the same length. A class in industrial arts may be more effective if it lasts for two hours and meets twice a week rather than for one hour, meeting five days a week. The lecture which comes before this session may be only thirty minutes.

The school day may be organized by half-hour modules of time which are combined to allow for varying lengths of class time. (See Chapter 5.) Attention needs to be given to the number of time modules comprising the school day; the length of each module is then set by the duration of the lecture, usually the shortest learning activity.

Experience has shown that it doesn't take as long to learn to type as it does to speak a foreign language. Teachers in the various content areas can, therefore, set the duration and frequency of meetings according to the demands of content and student needs. The recurring question is: How can students learn best?

In-Service Education

Any school which undertakes a team teaching program should also be committed to an extensive in-service education program, for team teaching implies changes in teaching behavior. Thus, it requires a full measure of time, practice and patience from all concerned. Teachers going into a team program need inspiration from administrators to want to go the extra mile in working on a teaching team. The teaching staff must feel free to operate in an atmosphere in which mistakes can be made, questions asked and attempts made again.

The in-service program must be included as a regular part of the year's calendar. Training for a team teaching program shouldn't be hit-and-miss, but planned and carefully tended. Faculty meetings can concentrate on team teaching discussions. The best faculty meetings are those characterized by staff interaction. When teachers talk to fellow teachers, the credibility index of what is said is high. Schools have found it a good idea to break into small discussion groups to discuss the promise and pitfalls of their team teaching enterprise. There is value in having a recorder for each discussion group and feeding the thoughts and sentiments of the discussion groups back to the faculty as a whole. The conclusions of these sessions are valuable clues to the administrators as to areas of further study and investigation.

Staff bulletins, both regular and special, are good channels for communication of new ideas and reinforcement of previously mentioned principles of team teaching. Teachers can best ponder suggestions and critically evaluate them when they are reduced to written words on mimeograph paper.

While the zenith of in-service programs is the extended workshop during a summer, many schools are financially restricted from this productive time for in-service education. As a result, school systems are establishing workshops throughout the school year to work on the development of team teaching projects. Whenever possible, released school time should be given to teachers for these vital professional activities.

Successful workshops in team teaching include maximum opportunity for the participants to discuss their feelings about the project and give ample opportunity for practice. It is not enough to talk about a high degree of student involvement for the students' small groups, for example, without giving the teachers an opportunity actually to practice the desired techniques. In one school the workshop participants agreed to tape a small group class they had conducted during the school day. During the workshop the tape was played back and the participants each made comments and suggestions about the strengths and weaknesses of the actual class. The tape recorder is a valuable asset to effective in-service education and teacher improvement.

The kernel of any in-service education program for team teachers is a sense of dissatisfaction on the part of the teachers with a current teaching technique or procedure. Healthy dissatisfaction is not based on a sense of hostility or inferiority, but stems from a constructive desire for even better ways to teach. Emphasis is on the "even." No teacher's personal or professional security needs to be disturbed by an in-service education program. Instead, the motive must be the lofty one of professional improvement through thinking, discussing, proposing, trying and evaluating.

The in-service program for team teaching must begin with the teachers' concerns about team teaching. Once teachers feel the idea has merit, and sense how they will fit into the program, the techniques of operation can be attached. The battle of the operational procedure is lost, however, if the teachers can't identify with the team approach at the outset.

One of the most promising in-service practices is the one of staff

Chart 3	
CONSIDERATIONS OF IN-SERVICE EDUCATION	
Content	1. Single subject area with specified content 2. Two or more subject areas with specified content 3. Single subject area with unspecified content 4. Two or more subject areas with unspecified content
Group Composition	1. Random grouping by administrative expedience 2. Special purpose grouping based on achievement, ability, vocational choice, personality, interest, ethnic group, sex or any other dimensions(s) 3. Grouping adjusted on an *ad hoc* basis as determined by the needs of the students
Size	1. Traditional class size of 25-30 students and one teacher—sometimes combined with another group or groups 2. Varying class size—large groups and small groups
Time	1. Single length class period for all groups at all times 2. Varying length of class period determined on a prearranged basis 3. Varying length of class period determined by the purpose of the learning activity on an *ad hoc* basis

visitation. When one staff member visits another and sees good instruction or a new technique, he is influenced significantly. The shrewd administrator will encourage and even structure visits of the staff to other teachers and other schools to see another teaching team in operation.

It is productive to send a carload of teachers to visit another team teaching school. Not only is the visit itself worthwhile, but the exchange of views resulting from the visit is influential in changing teaching behavior in a positive fashion. Adequate preparation should be given those who are going to make a visit as to what to look for on the visit.

Conference attendance is another way that team teaching is stimulated. When faculty members meet with other than their colleagues to hear presentations and discuss them over dinner or coffee, change is likely to result. The point is that teachers won't change their operation in a classroom if they aren't given ample opportunity to understand why and observe how new techniques of teaching should take place.

Structuring and operating the in-service program is one of the building administrator's most important tasks. He cannot leave it to others to do nor can he ignore it himself. Constructive changes seldom happen without a planned program for progress. It is through a sound and progressive in-service program that the building principal demonstrates his skill at educational leadership.

In some schools the professional development program is carried on by departments. That is, all the fourth grade or all the English teachers work on a problem together. This makes the study-action group small enough to allow for a high degree of participation. Other schools have used special-interest study committees effectively in implementing team teaching. In this case, the faculty is divided into problem areas for study and practice. Once the study committees have a feeling of mastery of their area, they report to the faculty *in toto* and discuss their findings. Again the method of organization for study committees should be geared to the requirements of the individual school.

The Staff Load

One of the more interesting aspects of team teaching is the opportunity it affords for lightening and even reducing the purely instructional load teachers carry. It is not at all uncommon for university instructors to teach nine to twelve hours a week. This load is considered a full one. The feeling behind the assignment of a nine or twelve-hour teaching load is that college professors need time for the research that underlies preparation and evaluation of student work. On the other hand, high school teachers have an instructional load of twenty-five to thirty hours each week. This leaves only one or two periods a day for necessary planning and evaluation. This is not enough for team teaching.

In contrasting the teaching loads of high school and college teachers, it is obvious the high school teacher must do less professional reading and give less time to correcting student work. Few high school teachers have time to meet with students in conferences to give individual help. The disparity in teaching load is not because college teachers have too much class-free time, but that public school teachers have too little and are overburdened. While a concerted effort must be made to reduce the pupil-teacher ratio of high school teachers, team teaching is no solution to unreasonably high pupil-teacher ratios. It does, however, allow teachers increased time for needed preparation and work with individual students. When one member of the team is working with a large group, the other team members are free to study, correct papers, prepare tests or work with individual students.

How does this time-saving system work? First, by defining roles in the instructional process teaching time can be conserved. For instance, if one teacher on the team gives the content presentation to the students in several teachers' classes, dual preparation isn't needed by those teachers on the same topic. A history teacher with an exceptional understanding of economics may give the lecture on one unit of work in several teachers' classes. Thus, valuable time is conserved for the teachers who do not have the presentation.

Another way of conserving teachers' time is by changing the amount of time students spend in class. If it doesn't take as much time to learn to sew as it does to learn science, for example, there is little reason for the sewing class to meet as often or as long as the science class.

There are several possible organizations of team teaching, each of which has a different implication for staff load.

The *teacher unit specialist* approach is the one most frequently found in the schools. This is largely due to the ease with which it can be administratively arranged. It requires classes of the same subject to be scheduled back-to-back (two classes of mathematics scheduled at the same time, for example). The teacher who is responsible for

Chart 4		
INFLUENCES OF TEAM ORGANIZATION ON STAFF LOAD		
Teacher Unit Specialist	One teacher concentrates on one aspect of content for combined classes or rotates from class to class when his area of specialty is under study. Others take different aspects of content.	Equal preparation and class assignments
Differentiated Role Specialist	One teacher concentrates on giving lectures, preparing tests, making assignments, etc., to large groups. One works with students in small groups.	Load varies; preparation time varies according to role
Informal Team Use	Teachers bring students together or go to each other's class on an *ad hoc* basis.	Equal load and preparation time

the content gives the lectures to both classes at once or goes to one class one day and to the other the second day. The members of the team can have their preparation periods staggered or the teacher responsible for the unit can meet with another teacher's class during the time the first teacher's preparation period is ordinarily scheduled. This means the teacher's load is excessive during the study of the unit of work he or she specializes in, but very light during the time the other team members are in charge of the instruction.

The teacher unit specialist approach helps lighten the load over the semester or year but it creates a disparity of preparation and class contact hours. The theory behind this approach, however, is that in spite of the disparity a teacher can do a better job with some parts of the instruction than with others. Also, teachers require less preparation for instruction in areas of the content specialty. Therefore, the students profit by getting instruction from the most qualified member of the team. The relief given (in the year) to teachers not teaching a unit will allow more preparation or give teachers a chance to work with students who are behind or ahead of the class group's work.

The *differentiated role specialist* concept is a more intricate organization for instruction. This organization calls for certain teachers to do all the lecturing; others work exclusively with small groups. The most learned staff members with particular verbal skill are assigned to the task of working with the large groups in content presentation. The other members of the team work with small discussion groups. All members of the team assist students during their independent study time.

More preparation time should be given in the schedule to the teacher who lectures than to the one who works with small groups. Although detailed depth preparation is needed for content presentation, it is impossible to prepare for a truly student-centered small group, for the small group is the learning situation where students question, express and internalize knowledge. The team teacher in the small group must clarify, assist and aid individual students as they think, discuss and question. The teacher's work is done on the spot and is determined by student statements of understandings.

The differentiated role specialist concept does not imply necessarily that one teacher's role is more important than another. It does recognize, however, that effective teaching requires multiple abilities and skills with one teacher possessing more talents than another.

The job of the small group teacher is by far more difficult to do well than the large group teacher's. Consider that not only are we accustomed to having teachers talk to us, but as teachers ourselves we are more used to advising than to listening to students. The job of the small group teacher—the knack of getting students to internalize content—is the most difficult part of the teaching process. Yet preparation time does not influence the small group teacher's effectiveness.

In the differentiated-role organization the teacher's load varies according to the functions he or she performs for the team. A teacher who presents content to large groups may have only twelve hours of weekly student contact, while a teacher who works with the small groups may have thirty-five hours out of forty for student contact.

The *informal team use* implies less formal organization of teachers' roles and does not call for a regular teaching load. The other two organizational patterns do, of course. Whatever the team organization however, it is helpful, even necessary, to schedule all team members for a common preparation period. This is not necessarily an additional hour, but the one all teachers have.

The informal team use is founded on the belief that teachers can join together when an occasion arises to share ideas or classes with resultant profit to students and themselves. Often the informal team use cuts across subject-matter lines while the other two methods do so less frequently.

Some informal teams are organized to include all teachers on one grade level. This is particularly true in junior high schools and very small high schools. Sometimes the English teacher works in a phase of the team work while the history teacher assumes responsibility for another aspect.

The danger of the informal team organization is that it won't have meetings and become operative, simply because the opportune time for action eludes the team. This approach to team teaching has few implications for the schedule of classes; its success rests on the motivation and spirit of the team members. The implications for teacher load are nearly the same as those for the teacher unit specialist.

Scheduled meetings of team members may be separate from or a part of the preparation time given all teachers. Like all assignment of teachers' time, the determinant of how the school's teaching talent is used is based on the motive of the person who makes out the school's class schedule.

Team teaching in itself is not a more or a less costly organization for instruction. The cost of any school's operation is determined largely by the pupil-teacher ratio, not by the use made of available teachers. The quality of teachers' work is, however, directly influenced by how the available staff time and talents are employed.

Fundamentals of Staff Morale

Team teaching, in each of its organizational forms, extends the tendency of our society toward specialization. Industry has specialists who buy or produce or market goods, since one person cannot skillfully handle all the intricacies necessary. In professions other than teaching, specialization is an accepted mode of operation. The architect plans a new building, the draftsman lays it out in detailed drawings and the field engineer supervises its construction. How few buildings would be built if the architect performed all tasks of planning, drawing and supervising construction!

Team teaching is an extension of the concept of increased quality performance through cooperative specialization. While it is relatively no issue to accept the rationale for team teaching outside the profession, it can be a different matter to get operational acceptance of the concept among teachers. The attitudes of those embarking on a team teaching program are critical factors in the eventual success of such a program. Accepting the rationale is a big undertaking for a teacher because it calls for a radical change in teaching practice and establishes new, however rich or rewarding, relationships with other teachers.

A constant eye must be kept on the morale of the staff of any school going into a team teaching program. Teachers must become accustomed to working in concert with another or others. On occasion they must be willing to act on the consequence of the judgment of others. Even more important, the team members must be willing to work individually in carefully carrying out their part of the team's work.

Somehow the self-contained classroom has insulated many teachers from the energy created when professionals talk about ideas in their field. The organization of the team means that each member is going to evaluate and discuss with another member the concepts in his academic field. For some teachers it is disarming to confront disagreement and differing views. While the outcome of disagreement and differences is beneficial in terms of better instruction for students, team planning and decision making can be an uncomfortable process. Those most troubled by team activities are the less competent teachers who resent the exposure of their professional or intellectual weaknesses to others. For these reasons a careful gauge needs to be kept on the morale of all the staff.

The approach to stimulating consideration of team teaching is worth detailed consideration. No teacher should become a part of a teaching team because a principal or department head has left the impression that being a team member will help eradicate a personal deficiency by working with a more expert staff member. Such a solution would go against anyone's grain. Instead, the administrator's motive in stimulating consideration of team teaching for every teacher should be the same: the improvement of instruction for students. Teachers who lack the academic background or the instructional skill to do a good job of conventional teaching will not be transformed into new teachers because of team effort. True, they may improve their knowledge or teaching skill, but team teaching is no device for transforming a loser into a winner.

Team members need to be given personal attention from time to time to help them get over the new road they are traveling. An extra question about the team's progress or a note in the mailbox expressing encouragement goes a long way toward keeping morale at a high level.

There is practical advantage in using the Hawthorne Effect to keep staff morale at a high level. The Hawthorne Study showed that performance was improved when routine was changed and attention was paid to workers in the Western Electric Company's Hawthorne plant.

The same benefits for school performance can be achieved when changes in school routine are made and when particular attention is given to members of an instructional staff. Because team teaching, at its inauguration, represents a deviation from usual practice, the force of its newness will give it helpful momentum in its early stages. Therefore, staff morale can be expected to be at a desirable level during the infancy, the first year or two, of the program. During this period the school's administrators need to help build a solid foundation of understanding of the dynamics of team teaching to sustain its use and effectiveness after the Hawthorne Effect decreases. Once a teacher becomes a successful and confident team member, the school's morale is on solid ground.

As pointed out earlier, team teaching can give the individual teacher increased professional stimulation and satisfaction as a result of contacts with a colleague about ideas, methods of instruction and students. Such stimulation and satisfaction is a morale booster. The exchange of ideas with another teacher and the feeling of accomplishment when a teacher verifies a contention with another teacher builds a sense of personal well-being and satisfaction.

Team members should be encouraged to concentrate on activities in the areas of their competency. Asking teachers to do things they are not equipped or able to do successfully affects staff morale most adversely.

Some schools using team teaching have failed to give the teachers' efforts widespread community publicity. This outside-of-school recognition goes a long way in cementing teachers' satisfaction in their work.

Of course, staff morale should be a recurring as well as a primary consideration for any administrator, regardless of the type of instructional program. Those good techniques of building pride and self-satisfaction in a conventional program have equal or greater application in a team teaching program. Any knowledgeable educator asked to list the five or six best schools in the state or nation will probably name the schools in which experimentation and innovation are going on regularly. One such list might include Scarsdale, New York; Mt. Kisco-Bedford, New York; Evanston, Illinois; Decatur-Lakeview, Illinois; El Dorado, Arkansas; Palo Alto, California; and Portland, Oregon. A complete list could go on and on.

Assumptions Concerning Team Teaching

At this point the assumptions which underlie team teaching should be clearly and specifically stated. First, while the general improvement of instruction is the broad goal, this is achieved primarily by the effects team teaching has on students and teachers. Second, team teaching influences the curriculum, the body of knowledge used as the substance of school instruction, the school administrator and use of the physical plant. As related to structuring a team program, the assumptions centering around each of these basic concerns are given in Chart 5 (page 48).

Influences of Facilities

Quality instruction and/or successful learning can go on in a barn or in a palace. The notion that team teaching requires a new building is nonsense. Some of the really superior examples of team teaching go on in very old schoolhouses. The most notable example is Newton High School in Massachusetts. Before the new high school in Newton was built to handle the overload of population, the operation of teaching teams was a reality. Although the new Newton School has mortar and steel arranged with team teaching in mind, the older building is in use and team teaching still flourishes.

Many of the older schools which have done superior jobs of making team teaching an accepted mode of operation do not contemplate new buildings. The emphasis on "flexibility" in contemporary discussions of school design to accommodate team teaching may have left the erroneous impression that a special physical plant is a must for team teaching. Such is definitely not the case.

The facilities which are needed for team teaching include:

1. team planning areas
2. space for large and small groups
3. resource centers for independent study for students and teachers

These can be carved out of existing spaces.

Team planning offices or areas are sometimes found in a corner of a teachers' lounge or in a specially designed room. While some newer plants have lavish offices and resource centers for each content area,

Chart 5

ASSUMPTIONS IMPLIED IN TEAM TEACHING

Concern   Assumptions

1. The Student   A. Increased learning can result through the coop-
                       erative efforts of the teaching team on a com-
                       mon instructional problem.
                    B. Psychological security can be established and
                       students will adjust to more than one teacher
                       working with a single student.
                    C. Interest in content can be increased as the re-
                       sult of team planning, presenting and structur-
                       ing appropriate learning activities.
                    D. Students profit from being in specialized classes
                       of varying size.

2. The Teacher   A. Teachers can work productively and in satisfy-
                       ing harmony with other teachers on instruc-
                       tional problems.
                    B. Improvement in teaching performance can take
                       place through team membership.
                    C. The opportunity for specialized and therefore
                       improved instructional performance may result
                       from team teaching.

3. The Curriculum   A. Learning experience selection, presentation
                       and student involvement are improved by team
                       teaching.
                    B. A broader and deeper body of knowledge is
                       potentially available to students as a result of
                       team teaching.

4. The   A. Team teaching demands special consideration
   Administrator   in scheduling students and teachers.
                    B. Evaluation of teaching skill becomes vital to
                       making decisions about the teaching team's
                       professional composition.
                    C. Team teaching, like any change in behavior,
                       requires encouragement and positive leader-
                       ship from the administrator.

5. The Facilities   A. Team teaching has space requirements which
                       must be honored for instructional groups, for
                       team activities and for the individual teacher's
                       preparation.

others have used storerooms, areas at the end of halls and a corner of an old library. When possible the planning area should be close to the instructional materials center and should provide separate places for teachers to talk, to type and to read. A room should be available for conferences with individual or small groups of students.

Spaces used for large and small groups vary considerably in both quality and arrangement. Some schools use the cafeteria for large groups and divide a traditional classroom into two or more small group stations. Other schools have built special rooms with movable walls and tailor-made spaces for each type of learning area.

Existing classrooms or study hall spaces are frequently converted to resource centers. Of course, modern buildings often house special areas for independent study.

Any school which has enough space to operate a traditional school program has enough space to operate a team teaching program. The new program may require a redistribution of activity areas or imply a redeployment of facilities, but it doesn't require either a greater area or contemporary architectural design. The teaching and administrative staff must first identify the instructional needs and then relate them to the existing physical facilities.

"Something there is that doesn't love a wall," said Robert Frost. Walls can be opened for entranceways or removed to expand areas for different uses. Minor remodeling can often convert an older building into an excellent facility for team teaching.

Once a team teaching program becomes operative, the space and use needs become apparent. Few school boards would deny building alterations when some evidence of instructional improvement is presented.

The contention that facilities are barriers to team teaching is more often an excuse than a reason for not employing the concept.

Public Exposure to Team Teaching

When a school inaugurates a team teaching experiment, care must be taken as to how the idea is transmitted to the school's patrons. As in all descriptions, much goes without being said unless a concerted effort is made to describe the new program accurately to parents and citizens. Too often the administration has not sensitized adults in the community as to what is being done and why. It can be devastating to rely on chance comments and delayed descriptions by students to tell the community about team teaching. Parents are more secure in hearing what the school is going to do before it is done, rather than after it is in full-scale operation.

A great deal of attention needs to be given to the explanation of what team teaching is not. It is not the college system brought to high school. Emphasis should be placed on the small group instruction and independent study to get over this hump. It should be further explained that team teaching is not only for the academically talented student; instead, team teaching is organized to give individual attention to every learner's needs, regardless of ability.

The school's patrons like to feel their school is working on self-improvement. If team teaching is promoted as the method to get at increased quality, support will follow. Parents should hear periodic progress reports from the school's professional staff on how the program is developing. A discussion of team teaching is an ideal program for a Parent-Teachers Association meeting, a board of education meeting or a service club luncheon. Some schools have used local radio and television stations for presentations of their team teaching organizations. Newspaper articles relaying human interest stories are valuable aids to community understanding.

The public wants to know, and then will usually accept, what is going on in the school. The effective administrator will develop a plan to get this job done.

It is unrealistic to expect continuing support for any enterprise which is not effective. This applies either to a traditional or a team organization of the school. Emphasis must always be on program development. Satisfaction and recognition will follow, once merit of any school's team operation is established.

CHAPTER 3

How Team Teaching Fits into the Elementary School

by

ROBERT M. FINLEY

Robert M. Finley knows the elementary school and knows it well, its problems, its promises. He was a fourth-grade teacher in Glencoe, Illinois, and superintendent of schools in both Ohio and Illinois; he was also a professor at Kent State University, Kent, Ohio.

Dr. Finley helped initiate team teaching in the elementary schools at Chagrin Falls, Ohio. At Barrington, Illinois, he supervised the building of new team teaching facilities, with planning rooms, movable walls, a centrum and carpeted classrooms.

He is well qualified educationally, with a doctorate from Northwestern University and work at several Harvard summer institutes.

A firm advocate of team teaching, Dr. Finley regards it as an excellent way to improve the quality of instruction in elementary schools.

THE RELATIVELY sudden advent of team teaching has caught many educators with their plans down. This technique has moved upon us so rapidly that the administrator can't always make up his mind whether to grab the next train or accept the more normal "let's wait and see" attitude. Some even decided that they liked the idea but that they would be smart to call it something else. So "it" became Cooperative Teaching, The Group Attack, Combine and Conquer and even Friendly Persuasion. No matter how thin you cut it, the fact remained that in the team process teachers worked together in a way that they had never tried before; and believe it or not, people liked it—even the youngsters.

With all the hullabaloo about this "thing" (team teaching), the emphasis was placed on the high school as the best possible area for the bout to take place. This was a natural conclusion since the departmentalization of the high school offered itself readily to any type of operational improvement. Someone felt that perhaps one teacher didn't know all there was to know about American history; and perhaps three American history teachers might do a better job in presenting the material if they worked together. So the die was cast.

Then one bright Monday morning someone thought that this team teaching idea just might have some merit in the elementary school—not the primary level, of course, because this area was sacred—but perhaps in the upper and possibly in the intermediate schools. Why not?

The Mother Hen, or Self-Contained Classroom

At the offset, let me say that the success of any high school depends upon how well the instructional job is done in the elementary school, especially at the primary level. I am also quite convinced that the teachers in the elementary schools have a better grasp of teaching methods. The movement toward the ungraded school makes sense and the methods employed by grammar school teachers have much to sing about. However, it is hard to see why these same progressive teachers fail to see the advantages of the team approach. They are the first to shout "Hurrah" for help in art, gym, remedial reading, music and speech, and at the same time turn their backs on help in their so-called "mother hen areas."

The self-contained classroom is an outgrowth of the idea that we should not break the little darlings away from their mothers too quickly. We fail to admit that these same children practically have been pushed upon the neighborhood all hours of the day and that the mother couldn't wait until Herman was old enough to go to school. This came about when Mamma was at a loss to know what to do with Herman.

That Herman was being influenced by more than Mama was very evident since he had practically terrorized the mailman, the milkman and other adults in the neighborhood. Mama, instead of being the mother hen, was more a source of refuge when Herman came home crying or to be fed. We act as though Mama has been the only influence on Junior. Have we forgotten Dad, little though he might contribute? Or perhaps that ugly black box in the corner which spills out Captain Kangaroo, Walt Disney or the baseball game?

I grant that the primary teacher has lived with the concept that she and she alone is responsible for Herman's education during that one year in her room, but isn't it just possible that she does not excel in all subjects? Isn't it just possible that one teacher is superior in reading and another teacher superior in writing? Couldn't these two team up, in which case the children might get the best teaching from each teacher and the least effective from neither?

I wonder why it is that some parents demonstrate a desire for one teacher over another as parents really are in no position to evaluate teaching. Why should some children "get" the so-called poorer teacher and others the better one? Isn't it possible some teachers are more adequate in some fields and not so hot in others? I think so.

Traditional Approach to Teaching

I am not advocating going back to departmentalization in the elementary grades. Nothing could be further from my thoughts. But it seems that we have been caught in a type of traditional teaching and thinking that says, "This is the way we have done it." Can't we at least try to look at the possibilities of how it might be done better?

I am quite aware of the insecurities that might evolve around sharing one's thoughts and guarded techniques with others. The outcome might prove disastrous to some of the things that we are now doing. Let's hope that it would. It might also upset a few teachers, too. This might not end the world, either, but might be the beginning of better teaching. Where security might have been lost in one instance, it might possibly have been enhanced in other instances as teachers saw that working together was a rather pleasant experience—done with the right attitude.

One of the main problems in the involvement of teachers with team teaching is that of breaking with tradition and the resultant difficulties in avoiding teaching performance insecurity. For the advent of team teaching was very similar to the advent of the ungraded primary. The problem with the ungraded concept, as with team teaching, was to unlock the thought in the mind of the teacher that she was no longer teaching a grade, but was now teaching individual children. This last statement smacks of Progressivism; nevertheless, there is a lot of food for thought here.

Advantages of a Team

Although there are disadvantages in team teaching, especially if the wrong people get together, or if the participants don't particularly want to be on the team, there are distinct advantages to team teaching in the elementary school. Some are obvious; some not so obvious:

1. The team approach offers the combined thinking of more than one person.
2. The team approach makes possible the "breaking in" of a neophyte teacher as beginning teachers can be teamed with experienced teachers.
3. The team makes it possible for more and better planning for the teaching of children. Additional planning time for the members of the team becomes available while one teacher of the team is conducting a large group listening or watching session. This type of program also makes it possible for the non-teaching teachers at this time to work with other small groups or individuals.
4. The team enables each child to "sit at the feet" of both the good and the poor teacher. (Let's face it—we do have some poor teachers, and sometimes twenty-five youngsters must endure them for a whole year.)
5. The team approach encourages ungradedness in the elementary school. (This is taken to be good.)
6. The team approach changes the outlook on recruitment of teachers in that instead of looking for a fifth-grade teacher, we now seek a person who has certain qualities that will enhance the team. Diverse personalities can be blended together on a team for the advantage of students.
7. The team effect on the child, psychologically, appears to be that many teachers are helping with his education. This is rather contrary to the belief that the child usually becomes disturbed, especially at the primary level, with no one mother hen. In a school in Ohio where we had a team teaching approach in an ungraded primary building without interior walls, an interesting thing happened. The four teachers working with 112 primary children in a "barn"-type building were also somewhat worried about little Henry not knowing which teacher was his. One day during recess, Henry came running into the small building yelling, "Miss X, Miss Y, Miss Z, Miss W, Willie cut his knee!" Now I admit that this little guy might have been so confused that he didn't know whom to

call, but I prefer to believe that he associated himself positively with all four.

The Building and Operations of a Team

There is too much thought that a teaching team, whether it be high-school mathematics or elementary basket weaving, is merely brought about by selecting certain innocent teachers who are ignorant of the situation and saying in an off-hand way, "You are now a team." This can't work very well. Probably the most important step in the creation of the team is the original step in team selection. The word "selection" is not the correct word. Before any team comes officially into being, much understanding and study should be initiated by the people possibly to be involved. First, they must have studied the various potentials of team teaching. In fact, it might be wise for them to try it experimentally. In one situation I worked with, teachers were asked to try an experiment. One teacher was asked to bring her little cherubs to one corner of the multipurpose room—and teach a regular day's lesson. The next day another teacher of the future team was asked to do the same in the opposite corner. And so on until all four teachers and their groups were in the larger multipurpose room. The next week we sat down with the four teachers and evaluated the activities. It was commonly agreed that we had created chaos. Some of the comments were:

1. "I couldn't teach reading when she was teaching music."
2. "Too noisy."
3. "I lost the attention of the children because they were watching the other groups."

Such statements were to be expected. When we asked why this came about and what might be done about it, we found:

1. Pre-planning would eliminate many of the annoyances.
2. An exchange of thoughts, as they occur during the day, would be valuable.
3. Daily evaluation and weekly planning would be valuable.
4. Even with the problems, the week was a success as far as instruction was concerned. Students were learning a lot and teachers enjoyed the experiment.

Many of the advocates of team teaching desire the hierarchy of operation. That is, there is a team leader and he or she is responsible for that team's success. I prefer the "change of leadership" within the team and the absence of the line and staff appearance for an elementary school. By this, I mean that some time during the day, teacher "A" would take over for reading, since she is the one on the team who knows the most about the subject, and the one who has initiated the planning. However, teacher "B" would take the leadership in the arithmetic area. This way, the leadership changes and the responsibility changes with it. Each teacher is both an Indian and a chief.

If there are key words in the formation of the team, they are *planning* and *evaluation*. This planning and evaluation must be consistent and candid. For too often the halo effect is upon us and we try then to procrastinate about the success of the team.

Space and Planning

Many educators have shied away from the team teaching approach due to lack of space or with the statement that the building wasn't designed for team teaching. It is true that if a building could be built for team teaching the results would have a better-than-even chance to succeed. But the building is not the main determinant for success of teaming. Too many teachers and administrators blame the structure of the building for the lack of interest in, and development of, team teaching. But many teams throughout the country are doing a bang-up job in old buildings. Where there is a will, there is a team. In many schools, the happenings at Jericho are repeating—the walls have come tumbling down. Flexibility is the password. Where two old rooms stood, the wall is ripped out and one large area now exists. Teachers can determine how the space will be used on an hour-by-hour basis. When a teaching activity requires a big area, it is at hand and when only a small area is needed, it is available also.

The pathetic thing about new buildings being erected today is that many—indeed, most of them—are in the image of the same old structures that existed in the early 1900's. There is more glass and more lively color, and it is usually all on one level, but the cells are still abounding. The only flexibility is to be found in the swinging doors.

Even disbelief in the advantages of team teaching is little basis for not building flexibility into new schools. Some may believe that team teaching is just another passing fancy, but there is little doubt that another fancy will follow, and another, and another. In order to meet the changes of the future—no matter what they may be—elementary school buildings must have built-in flexibility.

Changing Concepts in the Elementary School

"Change" is a beautiful English symbol. There is even something nice about the sound of the word. How we use the concept, however, is another bunch of bananas. For prevalent in the action of many educators today is resistance to change. Not only are educators prone to accept rigid thinking, but we also find it in the minds of the school patrons. Yet little do we realize that the only constant we have is change. Change will take place whether we like it or not. The question appears to be in what direction this change will come about.

I would like to discuss nine possible areas of change that, in my opinion, will take place in the elementary school. These changes are all developing around the concept of team teaching

1. *The self-contained class.* Where this concept once was "the thing to have, I feel that gradually we are shifting to the multi-person approach in the teaching of eager children—and even some not so eager. In order to present the best education to children, we must use the best in the education and abilities of many teachers.

2. *Better use of human resources.* This would imply that time and talent must be better employed in the education of children. Teachers must own up to the fact that they do some things better than their fellow teachers—and that they may be a rather miserable failure in other areas. Although this implies that a teacher must be a big person, I would not advocate that we go out and search for only big-person type teachers.

3. *Ungraded, non-graded elementary schools.* The long-existing graded school, such as first, second, etc., grade, has long outlived its usefulness to everybody except the administrator and state departments of education. It is true that it is easier to make reports that define 63 children in the first grade, 86 children in the second grade, etc., but educationally, this smacks of administrative convenience and certainly not quality in instruction. Maturation grouping must come about rather than so-called graded grouping in our elementary schools.

4. *The magic number is one, not twenty-five.* We have been conditioned to believe that a 25-1 ratio of children to teachers is the magic number for good teaching. This has never been proved. In

fact, we are finding that the only magic number is 1, just as the only miracle fabric is wool. Educators are finding that in some instances 100 or 200 in a group will gain the necessary results in a listening or viewing situation.

With the 1 to 1 relationship must come several changes in operation. First, the student must come to accept some responsibility for his education; and second, other methods of teaching will have to be forthcoming. I would hope that in the not-too-distant future we would have non-graded education, not from K-12, but for K-death.

5. *Programmed learning and automation.* Fight it all you will but it is still coming. Why? Because it will do the job and perhaps permit teachers to do some of the things that I have been chatting about. It will not destroy the teaching profession as long as we look at it as simply another tool that will help us to do a better job.

6. *The role of the elementary principal.* This is probably the most important change. No longer can we expect superior education without superior leadership. Universities and colleges must accept the responsibility for the training of elementary school administrators rather than we, who take an excellent teacher from the classroom and make him a mediocre principal.

We must also permit the principal actually to be the educational leader of his school. He cannot do this if his job is to count books, see that the snow is shoveled, keep the sinks clean or patch the roof. He must have the time to visit classrooms and join his teachers in the teaching process. His secretary must do much of the paperwork.

The principal must be given the time to be the educator, or the head teacher. In my opinion, he should meet with parents and other interested bystanders before and after school, not during the school day unless for an emergency. His time must be spent in seeing that better education takes place and in a quest to find out how each child can be given more and better instruction.

7. *Time blocks.* We must look at the elementary school day in relation to total time afforded for instruction. Shall we chop this time into relatively even pieces to make the schedule outside the door look neat? Or shall we look at each child and define large and small blocks of time in order to get a job done for that child? Can we say that all children need the same amount of time on each subject, as a state department may insist? We must go back to the time-worn proverb that each child is different. We should either

put up or shut up, and if each child is different and we should teach the individual, then isn't each teacher different and shouldn't the team approach be supported?

8. *Emphasis in the elementary school.* We must come to a decision as to what is to happen, call it objectives if you wish, for the children in the school. For many years we have gone along with the idea that the first few years are the get-acquainted years, the next few the get-to-work years, the next few the get-tough years, and the last few the "repeat, remedy and get-bored years." Rather soon we should emphasize that three immediate outcomes should evolve from the elementary years:

　　　　a. Primary − − − learn to read
　　　　b. Intermediate − − − learn the basics
　　　　c. Upper − − − exploratory years

These should be our goals for all youngsters, knowing full well that it will take a little more time for some and a little less time for others.

9. *Kindergarten role.* This area can no longer be termed the readiness part of the elementary school. Readiness is taking place in most homes for at least five years. The kindergarten must lose its name. I would suggest that the present kindergarten be called a part of the primary and that there be no kindergarten. In other words, elementary should be Primary (1-4), Intermediate (5-7) and the Upper (8-9). Note the elementary would now include 1-9; not K-8.

The term "kindergarten" implies too much so-called "readiness" or "let's play a year." Kindergarten teachers must be made to realize that they are part of the learning process and not the tool for merely getting kids to learn.

We must also take a good look at the school entrance age now being prescribed. At the present time we are permitting children to come to school if they are five years old by December, November or what have you. In other words, we are saying that a child is ready to come to school based on his chronological age. What a criterion for entrance into the formal aspects of learning! We should admit that this device is an administrative convenience but certainly not a sane basis for learning. Why not permit a child to enter school on his fifth birthday, no matter when it is? In this way, we could send the child a birthday card on his birthday and invite him to come to school in the following month. What a psychological birthday present! School must not be so bad after all, at least not so bad as Dad said it was. This technique would permit fewer children to enter the school at one time and would give the teachers a chance to study each child more carefully, rather than having the mad rush in September. Bugs in it? Certainly. But no more bugs than in the rather sorry mess we have now.

Where Is It Happening?

I would be more than remiss if I didn't point out where these ideas about team teaching are actually taking place. Who is doing something about it? Not verbally, mind you, but practically. I can find many people in the country who talk a good game, but very few who do something about this talk.

Naturally, you would assume, if you have read this far, that we in Barrington have something on the stove. You are right. The burner may not be up to its capacity, but the fire is going and the steam is up.

We have built two additions which are most usable for the team approach. These buildings are carpeted, have flexible walls, a team room and even a fall-out shelter which is wonderful for large group teaching. Our teachers are in the process of working out some team ideas. It is a slow process, but we are coming along. We are talking, but we are also acting. Other places of interest where things are going on are:

Lexington Public Schools, Lexington, Massachusetts; Chagrin Falls Public Schools, Chagrin Falls, Ohio; Glen Ellyn Elementary Schools, Glen Ellyn, Illinois; Barrington Elementary Schools, Barrington, Illinois; Pittsburgh Public Schools, Pittsburgh, Pennsylvania; Northeast Public Schools, San Antonio, Texas; Mt. Kisco-Bedford Public Schools, Mt. Kisco, New York; Saginaw Schools, Saginaw, Michigan; Sarasota Schools, Sarasota, Florida; Racine Public Schools, Racine, Wisconsin; Elementary Schools, Deerfield, Massachusetts; Park Forest Elementary Schools, Park Forest, Illinois; Carson City Elementary Schools, Carson City, Michigan.

CHAPTER 4

Potentials for Team Teaching in the Junior High School

by

EDWARD G. BUFFIE

Dr. Buffie is no stranger to team teaching in the junior high school. Currently he is curriculum coordinator of the University Schools, Indiana University. In this capacity he has been directly involved in the operation of a team teaching program.

Dr. Buffie served as a principal in Park Forest, Illinois, and as principal of the University Junior High School before assuming his present position as assistant professor of education and curriculum coordinator at Indiana University. He has worked with teachers in implementing new methods of instruction as an administrator, college professor and school district consultant. In addition, he is the co-author of a series of modern mathematics books, Sets, Numbers and Numerals.

Edward Buffie got his undergraduate degree from Northern Illinois University, his master's degree from Northwestern University and his doctorate from Indiana University.

TEAM TEACHING and the junior high school are like love and marriage. They go together.

The junior high school, the babe-in-arms of American public education, is characterized by its exploratory nature. In addition to mathematics, social studies, language arts and science, the junior high introduces students to an expanded program in the fine and practical arts, and almost always to a widened physical education program.

More often than not a venture into the realm of foreign languages is a part of the junior high program.

Diversity of subject matter during the junior high years (7, 8 and 9) enables students to explore many academic disciplines before plunging into the specialized curricula offered in senior high school. This period of adolescence, with its affinity for change and its expanding horizons, is congruent and compatible with the new instructional and organizational ideas implied in team teaching.

Team teaching has a definite place in the junior high school. When more than one teacher concentrates on an instructional problem and a consensus is reached as to the best solution, the teaching which results will likely be superior to what each teacher would do on his own. The wide range of content in the junior high program and the complexity of understanding the adjustment problems of junior high students make team teaching beneficial in the junior high school.

Frequently junior high schools are of such a size that they do not support a large staff. Typically, twenty-five teachers work in a school population of 500 students. The junior high teacher needs to approximate a "jack-of-all-trades" in each of his teaching areas. In this era of exploding knowledge, it is quite unlikely that an individual teacher can keep up with all facets of knowledge in his disciplines—in fact, keeping up in even one discipline requires perseverance. The inevitable gaps in knowledge which this human limitation produces result, of course, in weakened instruction. Team teaching, with its capitalization on the knowledge and skills of many, can go a long way in overcoming these problems.

As teachers begin to function together as a team, it is not altogether unusual for them to focus on the concern of class size. Large group instruction will quite naturally evolve as students are gathered together for testing, lectures or to view films. However, experienced team teaching educators are the first to point out that much of the strength of team teaching for the student is in the potential of the small groups. In small groups of ten to twelve, students can express, test, challenge, question and clarify concepts to a greater extent than in a traditional class of thirty.

But it is at this very juncture that instructional techniques prove most difficult. Most of us find it easier to lecture, or explain, or illustrate, be it in a class of thirty or a class of 150 than to stimulate a student-centered discussion. It isn't easy to get off the beaten path, particularly when one's experience and orientation have taken him unswervingly down the lecture path to instruction. To involve, to prod, to channel students in purposeful discussion and *problem solving* are very difficult tasks, but ones at which we must become more proficient if we are to get at improved quality in the schools. The importance of personal involvement in instructional activity cannot be overestimated, but we have very much to learn about how to best direct and stimulate this kind of learning.

Let's not make the mistake of confusing team teaching with small and large group instruction. They are not welded together by theory, but rather by prevalence of practice. Variations in the size of instructional groups is simply one of the many concomitant features that may be associated with team teaching. Such variations in class size occur because it has been established or proffered that in this way we can better achieve our over-all educational objectives or purposes. Varying class sizes, an organization for instruction where students in a given course sometimes meet in large groups of sixty to 200 students and on other occasions meet in classes of seven to twelve students, fits like a glove with team teaching. But, at the same time, the existence of a teaching team does not mean there is a requirement for varying the class size. Once a team teaching program becomes operative in a school, the next step toward adding instructional advantage may often be consideration of varying class sizes.

Composition of Teaching Teams

Team teaching in the junior high school can be organized in four ways:

A. All teachers from a single content field.
B. All teachers from a single content field, but restricted to a grade level.
C. All or several teachers from a single grade level, but from various content fields.
D. All teachers working with a narrow span of student ability on one or more grade levels.

The teams, once selected, may then be organized on either a hierarchy or equal status basis. In the final analysis, however, the total organization selected and procedures of operation must be suited to the school's personnel and to definite educational objectives. To adopt a particular pattern of organization without first placing it in proper perspective and seeing it in context is intellectual folly regardless of the height of its lofty motive. In other words, we should ask ourselves "What is the job we want to do in *our* schools and how can we best accomplish that goal?" This must come first rather than simply seeking someone else's likely solution.

Of course, any of the team composition types may or may not include services of non-professionals. Non-professionals can serve as instructional assistants to perform non-professional responsibilities: paper correcting, roll taking, visual production, bibliography typing, etc. A junior high teaching team can do work on a higher level if the team has the aid of an instructional assistant. Teachers should assume professional responsibilities and be engaged primarily in professional tasks. Quality of instruction must suffer when precious time, energy and talent are consumed in the performance of clerical details.

Obviously there are some people (and, like it or not, teachers are people) who cannot do some things. Not all teachers are equipped to operate in the same manner. What greater waste is there in using teaching talent than assigning a professional person to a role incompatible with his talent? Some teachers can't be members of teaching teams. There are many reasons. Some teachers have neither the inclination nor the desire to share ideas or to work with another professional equal in an intimate way. Still others do not have the ability to do so. Some have become creatures of their past teaching habits and cannot adjust to relinquishing control of "their" group to another teacher. Still others won't be convinced that working with another will have merit. The old saw, "He who is convinced against his will is of the same opinion still," has application here.

In full appreciation of these obvious differences, the wise administrator will not attempt to pull all teachers "into the fold." Those who are willing to explore the possibilities and opportunities made possible by an organizational structure which permits teachers to work together in new and wondrous ways—which they design and implement—should be permitted and encouraged to do so. The enthusiasm engendered by such professional activity and accomplishment has a way of spreading; there is a force of gentle persuasion which goes through a school after success of team teaching is recognized. Teachers with seemingly unalterable positions against team teaching often change their position when their colleagues have success.

Teachers and the Decision Making Process

There is no standard formula for team teaching in junior high schools. Each organized team, whatever its organization may be, has countless decisions to make which contribute to its unique character. For example, the background of the team members in terms of subject matter dictates what each member of the team will contribute. Personality characteristics of the team members markedly influence in what way and to what extent the team operates. Each of these elements contributes to the determination of the particular operational procedures used by the teaching team within the broad framework of the school-wide construct. The team members determine by their interaction with each other how positive the functional operation will be.

Junior high teachers have done a superior job in setting up team teaching guide lines, as evidenced by the work of the Lakeview Junior High School, Decatur, Illinois. No attempt was made at Lakeview by administrators to pinpoint specialized roles for each teacher on the teams. Responsibilities of the team members were agreed upon by the people who were actually on each team. While team teaching was accepted in principle at Lakeview, each teacher group worked out its own operational design. Reports indicate this was an effective and successful way to organize and, more important, to operate.

While the only real justification for any educational innovation must be found in improved education for children, there are many concomitant values in team teaching which may be associated. Not the least of these values is the professionalization of the teacher. It must be assumed that teachers, when functioning as teams responsible for the instruction of a large group of children, will have the responsibility and authority to make decisions relative to the education of their students. Decisions may involve such matters as:

1. Size of group to be instructed—large (50 or more students), regular class size, small or seminar type (12 to 15 students), or independent study.
2. Structure of groups—homogeneous groups based upon interests, past achievement, intelligence or needs, or heterogeneous.
3. Length of time to be devoted to work in given areas.
4. Nature of the curriculum—enriched, advanced or remedial work.

Team decisions should result in a more effective utilization of staff in terms of time and talents. A better educational program should result from getting the best and the most from each teacher for all students. This, of course, is based on the assumption that the members of the team can and will work effectively together and that their collective judgments will be better than those made individually.

Junior high school educators will want to consider altering the length of class time for each subject and for the group size and composition. The teams will consider how the curriculum should be adjusted to meet the academic needs of students. Teaching roles will then be assigned to fit the requirements of the learning activity. For example, in the typical junior high school United States history is studied in the eighth grade. With the team teaching approach, the first contact students make with the Period of Discovery might be a twenty-minute lecture followed by a sixty-minute discussion. The group may have 100 or more students for the lecture, but about twelve students for the small group discussion. The lecture may be presented by one member of the teaching team, while the discussions may be stimulated by other team members. The clock no longer dictates what shall be done; instead, staff decisions indicate what the junior high youngsters can do. Chapter Two presents the variables for organizing students' time and teaching teams.

Team decisions are based on professional perception of student needs. This precludes, of course, a school system's faith in the professional competency of its staff to make decisions about what is to be taught and how it is to be done.

Scheduling for Team Teaching

Too often we hear educators in the junior high school say they can't do this or that because the "schedule won't allow it." This is a weak excuse. It no longer has foundation in practice. Students can be scheduled into infinite numbers of groups for a wide range of purposes. Data processing can help educators take another look at schedule possibilities. By means of programs written for data processing equipment, students and teachers can be brought together in an infinite number of arrangements. Schools of the future will surely use data processing procedures to establish student schedules.

The limits of the school are bounded more by the imagination and professional judgment of the junior high educator than by the mechanics of scheduling. Schools actually committed to employing team teaching would be advised to engage a consultant who has had experience in the field of scheduling.

Scheduling for team teaching can be simple or complex, depending on the objectives of the school. The examples given below will show some of the schedule patterns available:

Type of Scheduling	Description
Back-to-back	Two or more teachers scheduled with different groups, but at the same time.
Unit-Specialist	Teachers move from class to class, and students' schedule is stable.
Varying class size	Large and small groups are regularly scheduled and teachers may have assigned group responsibility.
Block-of-time	Students are scheduled for designated blocks of time in set learning groups, and teachers exchange teaching responsibilities.
Ad Hoc	Teachers and students have no set schedule; class instructional groups are rearranged throughout the month by teacher decision.

Each of these offers opportunities for the teacher to bring students into contact with new ideas and different teachers in an interesting and helpful way. Different schools, with their specific objectives and differing local talents, will employ the scheduling pattern as mentioned above in varying degrees. The good schedule for any school is the one which gives the best advantage to students through the most appropriate use of teaching talent.

A school does not have to be organized into team teaching in all areas. Students can be given instruction by teams in some areas and in self-contained classes in others. Some schools have done a superior job of offering diverse experiences through team teaching to students in the practical arts, industrial arts, homemaking and business education, while others have employed the team approach in the academic areas. The seventh and eighth grade teaching teams at the University Junior High School in Bloomington, Indiana, for example, are organized on the latter basis. Each team consists of a teacher from the following areas: English, math, science and social studies. All academic subjects are taught during the first block (mornings); while foreign languages, the fine arts and physical education are taught in the second block (afternoon periods). Flexibility is the keynote—each team has complete freedom to use this block of time as their perception of class needs dictates.

The question of which subjects and which teachers should be involved in team teaching on the junior high level is left to the judgment of the building administrator. For a more detailed analysis and discussion of the administrator's responsibility in initiating and developing team teaching programs, see Chapter 9.

Successful Patterns of Operation

Some splendid instruction has gone on in junior high classes as a result of team teaching efforts. One school scheduled two seventh-grade history classes at the same time with two teachers (the back-to-back scheduling arrangement). When the content was in the area of greatest understanding and knowledge of one of the two team members, he gave the lectures, made out work sheets, developed discussion guides and constructed a good examination—one that taught as well as tested. The other member of the team took charge of a subsequent area of study. This arrangement resulted in better instruction for both groups since each teacher was able to spend more time for preparation, study and planning carried on while the other teacher was involved in large group instruction.

What were the outcomes of this experience? Both teachers, in a discussion of their work, were thrilled with the response in terms of positive learning products they got from students. The instructors attributed this advantage to the fact that their preparation and planning was more extensive and complete. Emphasis was put on involving students in reading, writing and discussing the topics being considered. Instead of casual employment of these procedures, the quality planning of these teachers insured richer instruction than was a part of the usual educational diet.

Another junior high team project of significance was one where the mathematics teacher and the science teacher pooled resources and class time to work on a unit of instruction in measurement. This was the teacher–unit specialist approach. Both teachers participated in the content presentation to all their students at the same time. One teacher presented the implications for science; the other gave the view from the content of mathematics. Both worked with their students in their regular classes on subsequent days. Herein lies another important value in team teaching. Oftentimes, stress is placed upon integrating subject matter because articulation between subjects makes for meaningful understanding in the correlated areas. Here again the teachers' evaluation was positive. The coordination of both science and mathematics was both significant and unique for these students and teachers. The teachers felt strength was given to the concepts presented by the two-pronged attack and by their cooperative efforts of integrating their content.

As junior high schools moved toward departmentalized forms of organization, much of the integrative quality of the self-contained classroom was lost. Through team teaching much of this can be regained once again with the added advantage of expertness in each subject matter area.

Schools using teaching teams composed of staff members from several content fields have lauded the advantage teachers have of pooling information about individual students. For the seventh grade teaching team at Indiana University's Junior High, this was one initial and important advantage recognized by the teachers. Since most of the students were new to the school, there was much to learn about the students before any significant decisions could be made regarding variation in class size, composition of class groups, time allocation and instructional programs (in terms of both content and methodology). The results of tests, individual student-counselor conferences and other teacher knowledge were shared and served as a foundation for the decisions which were later made. The assistance of the junior high counselor was invaluable at this point.

Teaming gave teachers a chance to contrast a student's learning ability and behavior in one class with that in others. In effect, teachers serve students in a much broader context, and better understanding of the student often results. This, the teachers felt, was also helpful to them in being able to give personal. aid to each student. Problem identification and diagnosis is necessary before effective solutions can be proposed and suggested. Often a teacher appreciates having a notion about the learning ability of a student reinforced or modified or even in some cases nullified. Perhaps the key to this enterprise is the team teachers' meeting time structured in the schedule and the administrator's concentrated leadership in the concern for individual student characteristics.

There is always a certain amount of interaction between teachers and an exchange of information about students when a particular problem arises, but the very nature of the team organization, with its emphasis on shared information about students, provides systematic consultation about each student. Problems are often stemmed before they reach the critical stage. Teachers can help each other as they work with every student.

Some schools have found it wise to include outside resource people on the teaching teams in the content development stage. One such school is an Evanston, Illinois, junior high school. A group of science teachers involved research experts in planning a unit of study in the scientific process. While the resource personnel, the consultants, did not actually teach, they worked with the classroom teachers in the team effort at the planning level.

One history teaching team in a San Diego, California, junior high school found the use of outside resource people was the natural consequence of attempting to get the best possible content presentation for its students. The team invited authorities to give the lectures of content presentation on California history. Also, ninety Californians got a first-rate lesson in political science from the local legislator. The teachers followed the presentations with class discussions and reading assignment.

The visiting lecturers in San Diego were willing and anxious to meet with the junior high pupils. They appreciated the opportunity of meeting with ninety students at one time, rather than, say, thirty. Once again, it was the combined thinking and planning of the teachers that resulted in this approach to instruction for a specific study.

The staff in one of the junior high schools in Newton, Massachusetts, has developed an ambitious program involving team teaching with the liberal use of independent study for students as also has been done at the University of Chicago Laboratory School. Already the advantage of the teaching team is documented at Newton after two years of operation. They use the *ad hoc* scheduling technique.

Junior high school educators would do well to give careful consideration to a worthwhile example of team teaching evidenced at Lakeview Junior High School, Decatur, Illinois. Here the teams are organized by content area on each grade level, grades 7, 8 and 9. The approach used in the Decatur-Lakeview Plan, as this program is named, involves large and small group instruction as well as team teaching. Matters of instructional concern, what shall be taught to whom and when, are carefully worked out by the teaching teams. The school operates on a schedule of large and small groups, but some 30 per cent of the students' time in the seventh and eighth grades is open for independent study.

Another approach to team teaching with an even more flexible schedule is the junior high school in Anaheim, California. Here the teams determine the schedule on a daily basis. Two days in advance of each class day the master schedule is redone according to the teaching teams' recommendations. This is an example of almost complete teacher control over a student's instructional day. Decisions about instruction are made in regard to the learner's need and are adjusted from day to day.

The kinds of activities just described are much more likely to take place as a team functions together and deals with its problems. We are the first to agree that there is no rule that says that one pattern of teaming is better than another. We must ask, "What will work for our junior high school?"

Too often we have heard that junior high pupils need the security of one teacher for each subject for an extended period of time. This contention, however, has not been documented by research or validated by practice. Students can and do learn effectively in a variety of environments without much threat to their basic security. In fact, a student's security is much more related to his acceptance by his peer group and his ability to handle successfully the academic demands placed on him than to instruction from only one teacher. An understanding and knowledgeable teacher can help in two areas: first, by knowing more about the student (his academic potential, past achievement, cultural background, etc.), and second, by adjusting the program to fit his needs more closely.

The Future of Team Teaching in the Junior High School

In order to understand better any predictive efforts about team teaching, it would be wise first to place the team teaching movement into an historical context. Over a hundred years ago, when the public schools were first organized in the United States, the self-contained classroom was established as the primary organizational basis for instruction. As children progressed up the educational ladder, it soon became evident that the classroom teacher could not know everything about everything. This realization led to the institution of departmentalized teaching. This plan was so successful—particularly in the upper schools—that it was advocated for elementary schools. At one time the departmental organization permeated the entire educational structure all the way down to first grade. But this was no panacea either. Now the child's learning became segmented—the integrative quality of instruction, the interrelationships of learning activities were lost, for the most part, and many educators became concerned.

In the late 1920's and 1930's the core program, led by the Progressive Movement, made its impact on the educational scene. In this situation one teacher was to teach in two or three areas of the curriculum. Presumably the teacher could integrate the areas for which he was responsible, whether it be social studies and English, or math and science. This seemed to be a more suitable type of organization since it apparently combined the best of both the previous programs. However, this proved to be relatively short-lived. Because of interest, skill, knowledge and training, most teachers had a tendency to concentrate on one area, often at the expense of other areas.

And now a fourth major development in this evolution has appeared in the form of team teaching. Team teaching has taken many forms, of which one of the most promising is the type of organization whereby two or more teachers work together to integrate more effectively their respective subject matter areas. Is it not reasonable, therefore, to expect junior high teachers to be very much concerned about this type of working arrangement, since typically their students have come from elementary school programs where self-contained classrooms lend themselves extremely well to the integration of learning activities?

If the junior high school is to serve as a transitory step between the self-contained elementary classroom and the highly departmentalized arrangement of senior high school, then a junior high program which combines the strengths of both is a must! The junior high school should be neither an extension of the elementary school operation nor a replica of a senior high program, if it is to justify and fulfill its existence as a separate and worthwhile unit.

When we talk about junior high school education for the future and what we hope to see accomplished, one of our deepest concerns is for the professionalization of the teacher. Team teaching presents the teacher with an outstanding opportunity to participate in the decision making process about students' needs and content. Team teaching presents the teacher with authority and a responsibility unequaled in other situations. With all the advantages the team approach offers to both student and teacher, participation in professional decisions about each student is one of the most important, and one which the professional teacher will come to appreciate and welcome.

As team teaching becomes a strong, vigorous element on the educational scene in junior high schools, we can expect to see significant curricular changes take place. Schools will move in the direction of a non-graded curriculum with complete emphasis on continuous education for all students. Then, when the curriculum is flexible and when scheduling is dictated by teachers, students will reap a great harvest of understanding and teachers a greater satisfaction in teaching.

The junior high school, the exploratory institutional element conceived in America, is a logical place to give emphasis to team teaching.

CHAPTER 5

Possibilities for Team Teaching in the Senior High School

by

EUGENE R. HOWARD

Following graduate study under Dr. J. Lloyd Trump at the University of Illinois, Eugene R. Howard became the first superintendent of Ridgewood High School in Norridge, Illinois.

Ridgewood is a four-year high school in which team teaching is practiced on all levels and in all subject areas. It has served as an experimental school for new ideas and concepts in education, and has been the subject of numerous articles and studies. As its superintendent, Mr. Howard speaks and writes authoritatively on team teaching in the secondary school.

Mr. Howard has been a speaker at national educational meetings and has conducted workshops for teachers interested in flexible scheduling and team teaching. Eugene Howard is, unquestionably, one of the outstanding administrators in the country.

Many new ideas are subtly at work today, quietly but quickly changing the serious high school. The typical high school of 1955 was not basically different from the high school of 1925; in fact, a student, were he to find himself transported in time from the one school to the other, would scarcely be able to tell the difference. His period of adjustment would be short and painless.

The high school of 1975, however, will be a vastly different kind of place. A member of the class of 1955, finding himself suddenly transported twenty years into the future, would not be able to adjust so easily.

If the forces now at work in education continue to effect the kinds of changes that have been made in the past five years, we will soon find ourselves with a new kind of senior high school having little in common with its remote ancestor of the 1920's.

A quick look at some new terms recently added to the high school educator's vocabulary will illustrate some of the changes in progress. When high school educators talk shop these days they discuss such topics as video tape recording, teleprojection, programmed instruction, the ungraded high school, the spiral curriculum, learning laboratories, materials resource centers, Q-spaces, independent study, education by appointment, movable walls and flexible space, language laboratories, flexible scheduling, BSCS biology, PSSC physics and SMSG mathematics.

True, some of these ideas are not new, and many have their roots in the school of the 1920's. But all represent forces for change—forces at work on today's senior high school.

It would be difficult to find a high school anywhere in the country not being affected today by at least one of these forces.

Needed—A New Organization

Badly needed by today's high schools is an organizational pattern into which these and other new ideas can fit. Typically today's high schools are organized much in the same way as they were in 1925. The basic organizational unit for instruction is the self-contained classroom containing one teacher, a subject-matter specialist, and approximately thirty students. Each teacher is responsible to a department chairman who in turn is responsible to the principal. The teacher is expected to serve the educational needs of all thirty students in his class for one year of work in a particular subject. Communication among teachers in a department is limited to two formal departmental meetings per month and any chance remarks which may be exchanged at lunch, during the daily coffee-break period (often called the "conference period") or after school.

Although we often acknowledge that students are different, we assume that teachers are the same, for they are given identical "equal load" schedules. Teaching jobs vary so little that it is usually sufficient to report a vacancy to the placement office simply by naming the subject to be taught.

Assumptions are also made, equally false, that the group size of thirty is equally appropriate for many kinds of learning tasks; that the length of the period, whatever arbitrary length the principal may decide on, is appropriate for whatever teachers and students may wish to do; and that everyone learns at the same rate. Likewise it is assumed that the self-contained classroom is equally appropriate for such diverse activities as lectures, discussions, supervised study, project work, movies and programmed instruction. In reality, of course, such a classroom is not completely appropriate for any of these activities.

The time has arrived when high school administrators are designing new organizational plans which are based on sound rather than fallacious assumptions regarding the learning process and the nature of individual differences. Administrators are at work renovating two of the most formidable impediments to educational progress—the table of organization and the schedule of the school.

Gradually it is being realized that the purpose of an organizational plan is to facilitate instruction. The school must no longer be organized primarily for administrative convenience.

The Teaching Team, a Basic Organizational Unit

The teaching team is gradually replacing the individual teacher as the basic organizational unit of the school, and, in some schools, departments, representing narrow, unrealistic compartments of knowledge, are giving way to broader organizational units.

One team teaching high school, the Wayland High School[*] in Wayland, Massachusetts, has only four departments—the sciences, languages, social sciences and the arts. Such an organizational plan encourages teachers to communicate with one another across the traditional subject-matter lines so that knowledge can be more easily related, correlated and integrated.

Dr. Lloyd Michael, superintendent of the Evanston (Illinois) Township High School, has recently described a teaching team as follows:

> A teaching team is a systematic arrangement wherein several teachers with a leader and assistants, and with an optimum use of technology, cooperatively instruct a group of students, varying the size of the student groups and procedures with the purpose of instruction, and spending staff time and energy in ways that will make the best use of their respective competencies.[†]

[*] Anderson, Edward, and Harkness, John C., "Planned Variability," *The Nation's Schools*, April, 1960, pp. 83-91.
[†] "Team Teaching," *The Bulletin* of the National Association of Secondary School Principals, May, 1963, pp. 36-42.

Effective team teaching, then, to a large extent depends on a successful analysis of three major factors: (1) the instructional task, (2) the respective talents of the participating staff members and (3) the physical facilities, technological aids and educational materials available.

Seven Basic Principles

The faculty of one team teaching high school, Ridgewood High School in Norridge, Illinois, has developed a set of guiding principles to assist the teaching teams in decision making as they analyze the task to be accomplished. These principles, called "The Seven Principles of Appropriateness," are as follows:

1. *The size of the group must be appropriate to its purpose.*

Chart I, "Variation of Group Size," illustrates one possible plan for a team teaching school interested in linking certain instructional tasks to appropriate group size.

According to this principle of appropriateness, the size of a group, depending on its purpose, may be as small as two students or as large as 300 students.

For example, the Ridgewood staff has found, in three years of seminar teaching, that effective discussion becomes progressively more difficult as the class size increases above sixteen students. For committee work or for interest-centered project work, the very small group of two to four students has been found to be most effective. For audiovisual-centered large group instruction, where team teachers have planned presentations appropriate to large numbers of students, the group size is limited only by the physical facilities. When the physical facilities are appropriate and the quality of instruction is mediocre or better, there seems to be little difference in effectiveness between a large group of sixty and a large group of 300. There is, however, a marked difference in teacher efficiency. Through large group instruction, team teachers can buy time which they can reinvest later in better planning or more individualized instruction.

The typical high school class size of thirty students is a maverick group size—not completely appropriate for much of anything. A group size of thirty is too large for effective discussion and too small for efficient presentation of material. The conscientious teacher who takes the principles of appropriateness seriously, when faced by a class of thirty students, would immediately take steps to correct the

CHART I

VARIATION OF GROUP SIZE

REPRESENTED ACTIVITIES	GROUPS	FACILITIES
Presentations 　Stimulation of Inquiry 　Enrichment 　Relating various 　　subject matter fields 　Building concepts 　Relating field of 　　knowledge to reality	**LARGE GROUPS** 60–300 **STUDENTS**	Large audiovisually equipped classrooms with fixed seating, little theater or divisible auditorium.
Discussions 　Forming opinions 　　based on knowledge 　"Trying on" of new 　　ideas 　Reporting experiences 　　with others 　Building attitudes 　　towards learning	**SEMINARS** 12–16	Small classrooms furnished with a round or oval-shaped table and chairs.
Programmed Experiences 　Listening 　Drill on facts or skills 　Learning at varying 　　rates 　Reading 　Writing 　Sub-group discussions 　Teacher pupil planning 　　and evaluation 　Experimenting	**LEARNING LABORATORIES** 15–60 Psychological group size 1–4	Large, open areas furnished with carrels, divided tables, and chairs. Carpeted. Listening booths, rear-projection devices, books, small conference rooms. Teachers' offices adjoining.
Interest-Centered Experiences 　Research 　Project Work 　Interest-centered 　　reading 　Viewing 　Listening 　Experimenting 　Conferring 　Evaluating	**INDEPENDENT STUDY GROUPS** 1–4	Library or resource center furnished with divided tables and carrels. Shops, project rooms, homemaking kitchen, laboratories. Community resources utilized.

situation. A large variety of sub-grouping methods has been devised over the years by ingenious teachers of conventional classes to enable them to sub-group students in order to provide better for individual differences.

2. *The composition of any group must be appropriate to its purpose.*

The organizational plan of the school must permit the staff, through analyzing the nature of the desired learning experience, to control the composition of the group. This principle implies more than mere "ability grouping." Many factors other than academic ability, such as interest, special competencies, vocational preference and emotional maturity, should be considered by the staff in determining group composition.

Also implied is that the composition of a group must be flexible. In an English class, for example, a number of students who need special work in grammar might be temporarily withdrawn from the large group, where the instruction might be inappropriate for them. Likewise, in any instructional area, provision must be made for special grouping of academically talented students so that they are not subjected to instruction in areas already mastered.

3. *The time allotments assigned to any group must be appropriate to its purpose.*

This principle has long been recognized in the scheduling of many courses such as industrial arts and laboratory sciences. Seldom, however, does the teacher have much to say about the length of time he will be with his group on a particular day. There is little flexibility in a schedule based on a standard period length. Most decisions regarding time have been taken out of the hands of the faculty and have been relegated to an arbitrary schedule.

One interesting effort to break the lockstep of time is being made in the Brookhurst Junior High School at Anaheim, California. At Brookhurst a new schedule is made each day on the basis of teacher requests. Brookhurst Principal Gardner Swenson describes the process as follows: *

> In planning the daily schedules, teachers meet with their team leaders to plot the program in their instructional area. They determine the material to be covered, the groups they wish to meet, the time to be spent on each lesson, and the method of instruction

---

* *The Bulletin* of the National Association of Secondary School Principals, May, 1963, p. 86.

desired; i.e., large group instruction, small group discussion, etc. This information is then recorded on a "Job Requisition" which each team leader takes to the team room to coordinate with other teams in setting up the master board. Requisitions are set up on the board, conflicts are ironed out, rooms and teachers are assigned, and the master schedule is ready to be transcribed and sent to each teacher-counselor for distribution to the students who will make out their daily programs from this schedule.

"The Brookhurst Plan" is only one of many efforts to give teachers more to say about the instructional situation. In Holland, Michigan, a new senior high school has been opened which was specifically designed for team teaching and a block-of-time schedule. The block-of-time gives the teachers more flexibility of choice regarding how their students will spend their time within the block.

At Stanford University, Drs. Robert N. Bush and Dwight W. Allen have successfully built conflict-free modular schedules with IBM computer equipment. A major objective of the Stanford project is to tailor-make schedules to the needs of teachers and students. The schedule is to serve, rather than restrict or limit, the instructional situation.

Approximately half the students at Ridgewood High School find themselves in the position of being able to schedule their own time for one-third of the time they are in school. It is not uncommon in that school to talk to students who have scheduled themselves into a project area for an entire afternoon of uninterrupted work on a project of interest to them. They may choose from fourteen different areas in the building which are open to them for independent study or project work during that portion of the day when they are not scheduled in groups.

Teachers, students and administrators can now look forward to making more and more decisions regarding time—decisions which until recently have been delegated to a rigid, arbitrary master schedule.

The time is now approaching when the master schedule will no longer be the undisputed master of the school.

4. *The physical and psychological environment must be appropriate to the activities of the group.*

Physical facilities form an important part of a student's psychological environment, but they do not constitute the whole of it. Special areas in the high school should be designed for special purposes.

One of the most formidable impediments to educational progress has been the building itself. The administrator who is seeking excuses for not doing away with the inappropriate and inefficient class size of thirty students can always say, "The walls are in the way." It is true that some P-TA mothers and quite a few board of education members might take a dim view of the administrator who, from time to time, sets a crew of men to work knocking down the interior walls of the school building.

Obviously, however, some changes in most buildings will have to be made if physical facilities are to be considered seriously as factors affecting the learning situation.

Planners designing learning environments must be aware of many psychological factors. One such factor is the concept of "psychological group size." This group size may vary significantly from the total number of people in an area. For example, a resource center furnished primarily with individual study carrels and small divided tables may seat as many as 100 students. Yet the largest psychological group size in the room might (and should be) only four—perhaps the four students who share a listening post or a conference room. The behavior of the students in this group might be expected to be more closely related to the group size one-to-four rather than to the size of the group formed by all the students in the room.

Once the physical environment of a learning area has been established, team staff members should turn their attention to some of the more subtle influences of the learning situation. Role definition is an extremely important step in the establishing of a new kind of facility. Students must know what is expected of them in their new role, and they must be assisted as they develop their concept of the roles of the team teachers.

For example, the teacher in a learning laboratory who projects to the learners an image of Simon Legreeism will have difficulty in establishing a productive area. An authoritarian, tin-hat teacher, attempting to run an area designed to promote self-directiveness on the part of students, finds himself out of place. The first thing he will want to do will be to rearrange the furniture into rows for better eye contact with his charges. Students will be confused because they will be reacting to conflicting elements in the psychological environment.

Another important element of the psychological environment is group expectations. The most effective seminars are those in which peer-group pressure, rather than the constant influence of the teacher, keeps the group productive. In such a group the student who makes an irrelevant remark, or who otherwise tries to sidetrack the group from its previously agreed upon goals, is soon put in his place by his fellow students. If the group expects productive behavior from all of its members, the group will be much more productive than if such behavior is demanded only by the teacher. This transfer of responsibility for learning from the teacher to the pupils must take place before much progress can be made by the group toward self-directiveness.

The student can gradually be encouraged to grow less and less dependent on a teacher as he learns to direct his own learning.

5. *The nature of a task assigned to a team staff member must be appropriate to his talents and interests.*

This is the principle of staff utilization basic to most recent school reorganization plans. The principle, long effective in business and industry, that no task should be assigned to a highly capable employee which can be done equally well by a less-talented, less-expensive employee, has not generally been accepted in education. Teachers, until fairly recently, have been so grossly underpaid that little concern was felt for their efficiency. But an administrator may be less concerned if he sees a $3,000-a-year teacher typing his own examinations than if he sees an $8,000-a-year teacher doing the same job.

A staff of professional teachers should be adequately supported by a group of technicians, such as clerical and secretarial employees, student assistants and teaching interns. In schools where a goodly amount of large group instruction is expected, the faculty should be supported by an adequate audiovisual staff, including at least one secretarial assistant to prepare overhead projection visuals.

The faculties of schools stressing provision for individual differences need to be backed by an adequate staff of competent counselors. The faculties of schools stressing the growth of their students toward intellectual independence need to be supported by an adequate staff of librarians. The faculties of schools where teachers are expected to do creative curriculum building need to be assisted in their efforts by sufficient supervisory and administrative personnel.

In the team teaching high school no teacher needs to teach in a subject which is not his major interest area. Furthermore, in the large group, where the talents of an entire faculty—in fact an entire community—become available to the teaching team, teachers are constantly teaching in those areas of their greatest preparation, and students are constantly exposed to the most competent teaching available.

6. *The nature of the supervision provided for a group depends on the nature and the purpose of the group.*

Supervision is the process of teaching students to require progressively less direction in the conduct of their learning activities. Effective supervision, then, is that which contributes to student independence and self-directiveness.

It should be the major objective of all high schools to graduate students who are capable of directing their own learning activities in their post-high school years. Such an objective is of special importance for the non-college-bound youth, who is most likely to stop learning very soon after graduation.

The faculty, then, must provide each group with the amount and kind of supervision it needs in order to be a productive group. However, it is both wasteful of teacher talent and contrary to the philosophy of the school to provide more supervision of a group than is necessary.

Thus, it may be expected that as a team supervisor experiences success in training his group for self-direction, he may find that the kinds of demands on his time will change. Members of a group well along the road toward self-directed learning will see their team teacher more as a consultant than as a taskmaster or disciplinarian.

In many schools, the amount of supervision assigned to a given group is determined, not by the maturity level of the top 90 per cent, but by the needs of the bottom 10 per cent. Failure to avoid this pitfall results in an expensive misuse of teacher time and talents as well as unnecessary spoon-feeding for students.

7. *The subject matter content must be appropriate to each learner in the group.*

One of the most important questions a student will ever ask a teacher is, "Why is this lesson important to me?" The teacher who cannot give an intellectually honest answer to this question which will satisfy the learner should examine his course content critically, attempting to see his curriculum from the point of view of each student in his class.

A well-planned curriculum is tailor-made by the teacher to the needs, interests and abilities of each student. Provision must be made for experiences in depth for those students who wish to pursue topics at some length. The student's intellectual curiosity should be stimulated. His "Quest Quotient" is as important as his intelligence quotient.

False Assumptions

As stated previously, most high schools today are operating on at least five basic assumptions: that all teachers are alike; that the self-contained classroom is equally appropriate for a wide variety of learning experiences; that a pre-determined period length can serve many purposes equally well; that the group size of thirty is appropriate for many different kinds of instruction; and that all learners in a group should study the same course content and should learn at the same rate.

Recent wide-spread experimentation has shown that these assumptions are false. Beginning in 1956, the National Association of Secondary School Principals, through its Commission on the Experimental Study of the Utilization of Staff in the Secondary School, stimulated experimentation in over 100 schools throughout the country.

Between the years 1956 and 1962 school after school demonstrated that: (1) schools can be organized in such a way that unique teacher talents can be utilized, (2) a wide variety of physical settings for learning can be devised which are more appropriate for some specific purposes than is the self-contained classroom, (3) schedules can be modified to provide a variety of period lengths for various purposes and (4) high schools can operate effectively and economically while providing for a wide variety of group sizes.

Breaking Lockstep

More recently a number of schools have experimented with variations in subject matter and methods of instruction.

Probably the best known of these schools is the Melbourne High School at Melbourne, Florida, a non-graded high school where students move through "phases" or cycles of learning instead of through grades. At Melbourne a student may move from one phase to another at any time; he does not have to wait until the end of the term to progress to the next highest level. Thus students may "escape forward." They are no longer held by a rigid organizational pattern in a group which they have outgrown.

"The gradeless curriculum at Melbourne High," says Principal B. Frank Brown* "is founded on an awareness that each of the school's students is different. The program of studies is designed to accommodate these variances in individuals."

Melbourne, to a large extent, has broken both kinds of lockstep that are currently retarding students' progress in many schools—the lockstep of pace and the lockstep of content.

Typical of much experimentation which has explored the use of

* Brown, B. Frank, "The Non-Graded High School," *Phi Delta Kappan*, February, 1963, pp. 206-209.

programmed materials in breaking the lockstep of pace is the recent Roanoke, Virginia, mathematics project.*

These studies involved 377 students in three courses—Algebra I, Plane Geometry and Algebra II. The students were divided into three groups for each course. One group was taught conventionally, one used programmed materials with teacher assistance and one used programmed materials without teacher assistance.

The results of the study were significant in at least two ways. First, the study demonstrated that pupil achievement can be "highly satisfactory" when achievement in mathematics is measured by standardized tests. "Programmed instruction," according to the Roanoke report, "through the use of teaching machines and programmed textbooks, has proved effective in providing for pupil achievement in and retention of high school mathematics."

Second, and perhaps most significantly, it was found at Roanoke that in the Algebra I programmed learning courses 72 per cent of the help classes and 77 per cent of the no-help classes completed the year-long course prior to the end of the school session. Similar results were obtained in the other programmed learning courses.

The Roanoke experiment is only one of many experiments conducted recently† which strongly suggest that the programmed learning approach can free large numbers of students to learn more at a faster pace than has ever before been possible. There is no longer any excuse in our schools for lockstep procedures which impede the progress of students who want to learn.

There is a danger that team teaching, because of the current widespread emphasis on the large group phase of instruction, will not be used as it should be to contribute to lockstep-breaking. In fact, large group instruction, if it becomes the central, basic phase of instruction, can be used to strengthen a new kind of lockstep. A lockstepped class of thirty students, each studying the same assignments and completing each unit at one time, is bad enough. The danger exists that schools will merely trade the smaller lockstep (group size thirty) for larger ones. The audiovisual devices in common use in large group instruction make lockstep in large groups attractive—even stimulating. We must not, however, use the large group instruction part of the team teaching idea merely to substitute a more pleasant inflexibility for a less pleasant one.

---

* *The Bulletin* of the National Association of Secondary Schools, May, 1963, pp. 114-117.
† Schramm, Wilbur, "Programmed Instruction," published by the Fund for the Advancement of Education, 1962.

A Team Teaching School of the Future

FOUR PHASES OF INSTRUCTION

Most team teaching projects to date have provided for only one to
three kinds of learning groups, and have therefore not been complete
team teaching projects. There has been a lot of cooperative large-
group teaching based on the "You talk and I'll turn the dials" method.
When combined only with conventional teaching, such projects offer
the students only experiences in two different kinds of large groups—
large groups of 120 students and large groups of thirty. That many
such projects proved to be less than stimulating should surprise no
one. Dr. Trump has made the point that limited gains only will be
realized from fragmented attempts at improvement.

The team teaching school of the future may be a four-phased institution (Chart II). These phases—large group instruction, small
group instruction, laboratory instruction and individual study—will
provide the educational setting for individualizing instruction and
breaking the lockstep of pace and content.

Instruction in each phase will be closely related to instruction in
each of the other phases, but the phases will not be lockstepped together. Obviously, if students proceed at their own pace through the
programmed units, the large group can no longer be used to introduce
material. As the large group instructor faces his class he must realize
that the students in front of him are studying a wide variety of topics.
The problem of the large group teacher, then, will be to select ideas
for presentation which will be appropriate for students of widely
differing experiential backgrounds.

Perhaps the large group of the future can be likened to one of the
more successful Sunday afternoon television productions which contain much significant educational material. This material is usually
presented to people of widely differing educational backgrounds.
The more successful large group presentations will probably be con-
cept-centered, and the teacher will be seen gradually building each
concept by reference to experiences which students have had or
which can be understood by students. For this concept-building he
may use illustrations from the community, real objects, demonstrations, students' projects from independent study, slides, movies or
tape recordings.

For example, a teacher whose objective is to show that art, music
and literature are all means of communicating emotion might use a
combination of real people, perhaps the art and music teachers, a
sound motion picture, illustrating the relationship of music and art,

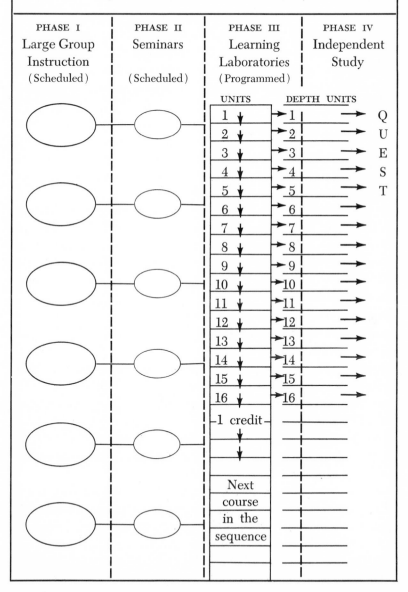

CHART II

ORGANIZATION PLAN OF COURSE STUDY
FOR A TEAM TEACHING HIGH SCHOOL

(FOUR PHASES OF INSTRUCTION)

PHASE I	PHASE II	PHASE III	PHASE IV
Large Group Instruction (Scheduled)	Seminars (Scheduled)	Learning Laboratories (Programmed)	Independent Study

UNITS   DEPTH UNITS

1 → 1 → Q
2 → 2 → U
3 → 3 → E
4 → 4 → S
5 → 5 → T
6 → 6 →
7 → 7 →
8 → 8 →
9 → 9 →
10 → 10 →
11 → 11 →
12 → 12 →
13 → 13 →
14 → 14 →
15 → 15 →
16 → 16 →

1 credit

Next
course
in the
sequence

Students progress at their own rate through a series of units and through a sequence of courses. Provision is made for variation of content, for depth study and for interest-centered activity.

slides of great paintings, a tape recording of Carl Sandburg reading a portion of "The People, Yes" and an overhead projection diagram showing some of the characteristics of human emotion.

In addition to being used for inductive concept building, as suggested above, large group instruction in the school of the future will have many other valuable contributions to make to the educational program. It will be used regularly, for example, for relating fields of knowledge to the real, everyday world of business, industry, education or community affairs. Community consultants will frequently be used by the school to contribute to this objective. Large groups will also prove valuable for stimulating inquiry and project work, enrichment and the relating of subject matter fields through correlation of integration.

THE LEARNING LABORATORY

Much is now known about how a learning laboratory should function. Foreign language laboratories have been used for a number of years to enable students to learn at varying rates. Likewise, a considerable amount of experimentation has gone into reading laboratories, which now have become common in both elementary and secondary schools. A few business education and mathematics laboratories have been established experimentally. A learning laboratory has been functioning for a number of years at Wahlquist Junior High School, Ogden, Utah. An excellent learning laboratory forms the central facility of the Encyclopaedia Britannica School in Chicago.

A learning laboratory differs from a library or a resource center in that the learning laboratory is designed primarily to accommodate assignment-centered activities which have been built into a program. This program should include different kinds of activities—not just those which are typically associated with teaching machines. As a student works his way through a unit assignment sheet he should find himself engrossed in varied activities: reading, writing, listening, conferring with other students and with his teacher, viewing, solving problems, experimenting and evaluating.

A unit of study, the basic organizational unit of a learning laboratory course, consists of a carefully planned series of experiences designed to produce a pre-determined educational result. Alternate units and operational depth units can be planned, if desired, to provide for differentiation of content as well as pace. A student may stop work on the programmed material at any time, with his teacher's permission, in order to pursue an independent study project. Some students will undoubtedly complete the course of study and receive the unit's credit before the school year ends. When a student has completed a unit of work, he may be offered several options such as: (1) proceeding with the next course and completing some of the units in the more advanced sequence, (2) planning an independent study project or (3) choosing a depth study unit previously bypassed.

In addition to offering the advantage to the learner of flexibility of pace and content, the learning laboratory encourages independent study, provides each student with a variety of experiences which can form the basis for sound discussion in the seminar, encourages teacher-pupil planning and education by agreement and provides for a highly efficient learning situation for basic material. In the learning laboratory, advancement from one unit to another is on the basis of demonstrated competence only. It is almost impossible for a student to fail; however, some students will succeed more rapidly than others.

The Seminar

The discussion method has found widespread acceptance by teachers of all subject-matter fields over the years. Much valuable teaching is done through discussion in practically every high school in the country. The seminar in the team teaching school is designed to enable teachers to do a better job of stimulating discussion by providing a more appropriate group size and learning environment.

The seminar is the scheduled, structured discussion group. Much discussion will also take place elsewhere in the school—in conference rooms in the learning laboratories, for example, or informally in the student commons. The seminar, however, should be planned and structured to achieve a predetermined purpose. The teacher of such a group should participate but should not dominate the group. His function is to guide the discussion, to stimulate students to think deeply and consider the basis of their opinions carefully and to serve as a resource person for the group. The most important function of the teacher in the seminar is a subtle one: he must help the group establish the kind of psychological learning environment which will enable the group to function effectively even though the group may not be dominated by the teacher.

The seminar, properly taught,* can provide students with a unique opportunity to build concepts and opinions on the basis of knowledge. The seminar provides each student with a ready-made critical audience as he "tries on" various ideas. It provides a forum for the ex-

---

* For a further discussion of seminar methodology see: "Why Seminars Don't Work," *School Management*, June, 1962,, pp. 51-54 and Kable, Dolores, "A Look into the Seminar," *Clearing House*, May, 1963, pp. 557-559.

change of experiences, enabling students to relate ideas presented in the large group to their experiences in independent study or in the learning laboratory. It provides a unique setting for the guided and planned discussions of controversial issues.

INDEPENDENT STUDY

Independent study in most senior high schools takes the form of optional outside reading, special reports based on reading or experimentation, project work or the pursuing of courses of study not in the regular curriculum for advanced placement. Independent study typically takes place in the library, in project rooms or in laboratories or shops. A student's independent study advisor may or may not be one of his regularly assigned teachers. He may, in fact, be a resource person from the community who is not a regular faculty member.

In the high school in which the basic organizational unit is the lockstepped class of thirty students, independent study is extremely difficult. A teacher may, as frequently happens, build an "escape hatch" into his class of thirty, thus allowing students interested in independent study to pursue their quest. The disadvantage of "escape hatching" is that the student, while absent from class, is likely to miss the presentation of some important material and certainly will miss much of the discussion which forms an important part of every unit of instruction. If he chooses to make up the work he has missed, he finds himself burdened with a double work load—his independent study project and his make-up work. If he does not make up the work, he may find himself with gaps in his education. Thus "escape hatching" to provide for independent study forces the student to choose between two equally unpleasant penalties.

If the student chooses to do his independent study outside class time, he has not improved his situation much. He usually finds that the work must be done after school or during the day at a time when his advisor is not available. And regardless of when it is done it must be done in addition to the regularly assigned work.

Under such circumstances it is surprising that there is as much independent study in the schools as there is. The organizational structure of the typical school usually discourages such activity.

In the team teaching school where the learning laboratory is the central phase of instruction, independent study will be strongly encouraged. In such a school, at the end of each unit of instruction, a student may choose: (1) to continue with the program, progressing to the next unit, (2) to elect one or more depth units or (3) to leave the program and engage in independent study.

If he chooses to leave the program for independent study, the next unit of instruction will be waiting for him after his project has been completed. He has no make-up work to complete and no gaps in his education. He simply continues in the sequence where he had left it before being released for independent work.

When appropriate, independent study units can, at the discretion of the teacher, be accepted for credit in place of certain units in the regularly planned sequence.

Almost every student should, from time to time, engage in independent study, but some students will benefit from this phase of instruction more than will others. The schedule of the school must make time available to students for independent study appropriate to each student's level of maturity. For in many schools, the student least able to accept responsibility for his own learning is usually the one who elects the fewest subjects and finds himself with the most study time. Schedules for less responsible students should be tailor-made for their needs, so that they do not find themselves with more independent study time in their schedule than they are capable of handling.

IMPEDIMENTS TO PROGRESS

There are, of course, a number of reasons why this ideal team teaching school of the future may be quite long in arriving. Nevertheless, the potential is there. Enough is known about how to plan, build and operate such a school, so it could be built immediately.

The principal impediment to progress is fear. In too many school districts where we are trying to teach students to face the future with confidence, everyone seems to be afraid of everyone else. The teachers are afraid of their principal; the principal is afraid of his superintendent; the superintendent is afraid of the board; and the board is afraid of the community. The students stand alone; they aren't afraid of anybody.

Another formidable impediment is the Carnegie Unit and other unreasonable methods of measuring students' progress in terms of time spent by students in groups. Regional accrediting organizations are now at work on the Carnegie Unit problem and can be expected to arrive at some reasonable solution soon.

There is always, of course, the impediment of money. Very little in education can be improved without the expenditure of at least a little "pump priming" money to get projects started. All indications are, however, that the team teaching school of the future will be more efficient and hence not more expensive to operate than would conventionally organized high schools.

CHAPTER 6

Procedures for Inaugurating Team Teaching

by

ROBERT W. JONES

Educated at Indiana University, Bloomington, Indiana, Robert W. Jones was a high school principal before becoming Assistant Director of the Foreign Relations Project of the North Central Association of Colleges and Secondary Schools. In this position Mr. Jones visited schools all over the United States, conducting workshops and assisting teachers and administrators to improve their educational practices.

Earlier he helped in a study of team teaching financed by the Ford Foundation and conducted by the National Association of Secondary School Principals' Commission on Staff Utilization.

He is currently serving as principal of the Penn High School in Mishawaka, Indiana.

Both theoretically and practically Mr. Jones knows team teaching and the procedures it necessitates.

IF TEAM TEACHING is to become a reality, attention must be focused on the process by which change is brought about in a school.

The first commitment to team teaching must be on the verbal level. Teachers need to believe that working with other teachers will yield mutual advantage to students and themselves.

Once teachers have verbalized the desire to become part of team teaching, they must develop the operational ability to team teach; and here lies the major obstacle in launching a team teaching program.

In the current emphasis on educational innovation, a marked imbalance exists between the verbal and the operational levels of action. One need only read reports of what some schools claim to be accomplishing and then visit their classrooms to see that a dichotomy exists between theory and practice.

The method of team teaching decided on determines the method required to inaugurate the program. For example, a school deciding to use team teaching throughout all grade and curricular areas will need a much more elaborate plan of implementation than a school planning to team teach on a limited basis.

As the pace of change in education quickens, the means by which new programs are made operational becomes more important. Educators almost universally repeat the truism that curriculum changes only as teachers change, yet only isolated programs reflect evidence of this principle. Before launching a team teaching program, or any other new practice, careful consideration should be given as to how the desired change will be realized.

Let's consider team teaching specifically. The operational phase of change is first determined by the degree of verbal commitment to the concept. But the degree of verbal commitment can be of no appreciable and lasting benefit until its impact directly affects the manner in which students are taught. The question is not whether innovation is necessary to revitalize instruction once there is commitment on the staff's part, but rather what the nature of the changes should be.

Ingredients of Change

As every chef has his own deviation from a standard recipe, the ingredients of change vary according to the innovator. Study of schools inaugurating team teaching quickly reveals that no single path to success is available. Every recipe has some basic ingredients; likewise, there are common elements to be found in educational change.

An ever present ingredient in the recipe of change is its occurrence within the context of human behavior. Change in teaching procedures implies altering human behavior, a most complex and challenging task. Unfortunately, in most instances teachers resist change, particularly if any reasonable level of success has been attained in the previous way of instructing.

The more the team teaching proposal will deviate from present behavior, the more formidable the undertaking to bring about change. If human behavior is to be altered, sufficient reason must be provided to convince the teacher that change is necessary and desirable. This is the administrator's responsibility.

There are ways in which the team teaching innovator can channel group behavior to specific ends. In theory it is undesirable to manipulate people, but in practice it is often necessary. For example, group commitment obtained through the democratic process is a potent weapon in implementation of a team program. Once committing himself in democratic group discussion to the advantages of teaming, the individual teacher will feel obligated to lend some support in making team teaching a success. Then, the implementor can recapitalize on faculty and professional meetings, study groups, P.-T.A. programs and workshops to provide ample opportunity for verbal interaction toward the purpose of gaining group commitment to the team teaching concept.

Another method to influence change of human behavior via democratic means is to give a group special attention. Industry learned long ago that special attention directed toward a group is most effective in increasing efficiency and output. The implication here is to develop an attitude within the group that there is something special about what they are doing. Given special attention, a group of teachers generates enthusiasm and team teaching automatically becomes important to those involved.

In mapping strategy for change, the innovator should appraise his plans from the point of view of how others involved in implementation will accept the approach. By attempting to gain insights into how others are most likely to feel and react toward any proposed change, better provision can be made to accommodate the dimensions of human behavior.

On the operational level, teachers should be given the opportunity to discuss team roles in faculty meetings, opportunity to give lessons before the faculty for critical (what is strong as well as weak) study, and exposure to frequent supervisory visits. Teachers profit and respond favorably to supportive class visits by administrators. Follow-up conferences are necessary, however, for the value of the visit to come to its fruition.

A necessary and primary ingredient for successful implementation of team teaching is developing within the school a climate that is favorable for change. Innovation is not likely to occur if the tone of the school encourages rigid conformity to traditional patterns of instruction, since all school personnel must be willing to place a premium on the search for promising ideas for improving existing instructional practices. A healthy dissatisfaction with traditional teaching procedures is vital. All that is old should not be considered obsolete, and age alone should not grant sanctity. If the administrators equate conformity to traditional methods with good teaching, there can be little real hope of placing a school in the mainstream of educational innovation in the direction of team teaching.

The climate for change will be determined by the manner in which administrators either recognize or ignore teachers' attempts at meaningful instructional experimentation, however slight that experimentation may be. And by encouraging responsible innovation in every classroom, the administrator can be a strong force in promoting a climate favorable to change.

An interesting contrast is apparent in the success of industry in providing for progress and the slow, unsteady pace of schools in solving the dilemma of change. Industry has a built-in provision for and commitment to innovation. Research, development and retooling departments are important areas in industry. In many sectors of manufacturing the ability to change rapidly is the very price of survival. Funds are budgeted to provide for orderly investigation and adoption of new systems and procedures, and the unprecedented status held by the researcher in today's industrial world attests to the importance placed on the search for new and better ways.

On the other hand, the schools appoint curriculum committees to investigate, plan and carry out change on an after-hours basis. In most instances there is no effective mechanism for systematically reviewing and evaluating significant national efforts toward change or introducing improvements into the local program. All stimuli for new ideas usually come from the faculty and are developed while the staff carries a full teaching load.

Until change becomes a commitment of those directly responsible for the educational policy of schools, there is little likelihood that widespread innovation with long range and lasting impact can occur. Change must be considered an opportunity to invest in the future, not a cost or obligation forced on the school. Administrators must find time, materials and funds to help teachers test their notions about team teaching; for schools, like industry, must recognize the price of progress.

Both those involved in initiating change and personnel charged with carrying it out at the operational level must be accorded reasonable security to carry on such work. Any proposal for change should receive careful screening as to its probability for success and improvement of instruction, but a margin of error must also be allowed for those instances when teachers prove unable to make the contribution expected. Inherent in change is the fact that occasionally the change will not bring about the desired result. But experiments that fail can be successful if they serve as a basis of what not to do in the future.

Strategy for Change

Sanction to attempt innovation is a foremost ingredient of change. Approval must be secured from teachers, students, boards of education and the school's patrons. In some respects this sanction might not be considered an ingredient so much as a process by which what will be attempted is determined.

If the schools are a reflection of the community they serve, the sanction to attempt innovation extends beyond the formal channels of decision making within the school's walls. Change concerns all sectors of the community; it is a blending of the professional judgment in the schools with community expectations. While the degree of their influence and participation varies, each group in the school community has a role to play in the change process. So interrelated are their roles that at any time a sufficient breach occurs betweeen the school and community, innovation is doomed and progress is impossible.

In his study *Organizing New York State for Educational Change*, Henry Brickell[*] identified the roles of school-community groups as related to their roles in change as follows:

1. Parents' and citizens' groups in most communities do not exert a direct influence on the adoption of new types of instructional programs, but their influence is decisive when exerted.
2. The board of education in most communities is not a strong agent in determining the path of educational innovation, but its influence is decisive when exerted.
3. New types of instructional programs are introduced by administrators. Contrary to general opinion, teachers are not change agents for instructional innovation of major scope.
4. Classroom teachers can make only three types of instructional change in the absence of administrative initiative: (*a*) change in classroom practice, (*b*) relocation of existing curriculum content, and (*c*) introduction of single courses at the high school level.

[*] Brickell, Henry M., *Organizing New York State for Educational Change* (Albany: New York State Education Department, 1961), pp. 20-26.

Realistic recognition of the politics involved in gaining acceptance for team teaching places the administration at the matrix of the change process. By virtue of its leadership status, avenues of communication with the community and its special relationship with the board of education, the administration must serve as the nucleus of innovation. The administration must weld together the many elements influencing the school so as to provide common direction to innovation.

The real test of administrative effectiveness is its ability to obtain sanction from the board of education, interpret the program to the public and translate the change into operational practice. The success of implementing team teaching will be directly proportional to the leadership ability and commitment of the local school administration.

Since the ultimate success of team teaching will be determined by the skill with which teachers apply this innovation, emphasis during preparation for implementation must focus on instructional personnel. They need sufficient opportunity and psychological support to develop a working rationale for team teaching and to obtain new skills necessary for the change.

The implementation process indicates the need for instructional as well as administrative leadership for an effective transition to team teaching. Again, the administration is pivotal because it builds the framework within which the faculty will operate. Maximum impact to instructional leadership is possible only when it functions with positive administrative support. Additionally, the commitment of certain key teachers should not be underestimated as a potent force in making team teaching operational within a school.

Individuals almost invariably exert greater influence on change than groups or institutions. Individuals influence the decisions of groups and institutions, and the leadership of certain personalities is just as vital in providing purpose and direction in each school setting.

The process of change is impaired if a leadership void exists either in the administrative realm or in key instructional positions. The absence of leadership, or obstructionist tactics on the part of key teachers can pose serious problems to the implementor.

Leadership exists for the purpose of guiding and giving direction to the group, not relinquishing all authority to the group. Administrative leadership cannot be delegated. Democratic participation and giving the individual a voice in the decision making process makes group action more binding, but it is not a substitute for leadership itself.

The Change to Team Teaching

If one broad contrast can be drawn between team teaching and other current innovations, it is that team teaching requires changing the manner in which the school organizes for instruction. In other proposals the school's organizational structure is incidental to innovation, but it is the central focus of the change to team teaching. Team teaching implies utilizing teachers' time and talents in varying class sizes determined by the instructional task. Increasing the total organizational flexibility is a basc tenet of team teaching. However, the most unchanging part of the school has been its organizational structure; thus, team teaching proposes to alter what historically has been the most stable part of the school. From time to time schools change course content; team teaching, though, represents a wholesale alteration of how courses are taught.

The revolution in staff relationships brought about by team teaching is that faculty members no longer function within the context of individual classrooms; instead, they combine efforts to operate as a corporate entity. Functioning as just one part of a corporate entity is a major adjustment required of teachers changing to team teaching. Changing the self-image from the traditional to the corporate will be a difficult transition for some teachers. Implementation must concentrate on helping teachers perceive their new role as part of a unified instructional effort. The present relative isolation of the teacher is reduced in team teaching, and ample opportunity must be given for the team to accustom itself to the new context in which it operates.

In giving teachers experience in working together, there is no substitute for group discussion. The teachers who will constitute a team should actually develop their first teaching unit as a group early in the preparation for team teaching. By stressing this process many valuable insights are gained.

No discussion of team teaching can escape the question of its probable effect on students. Research indicates it is no worse than traditional teaching; however, proponents of team teaching are quick to indicate that present teaching devices do not adequately evaluate the added instructional depth that team teaching provides.

Two problems of team teaching that should be anticipated are the possibility of impersonality in instruction and the difficulty of some students in adjusting to team teaching. Preparation for implementation must reduce both problems to a minimum. Planning team teaching to include individualized instruction and developing teachers' responsibility for individual learning will preclude the danger of impersonality.

A pre-program education of students as to the purposes and advantages of team teaching will help them adjust to it. Articles in the school newspaper, student council discussions and convocations on team teaching will bring about a smooth transition. If team instruction actually provides more opportunities for varying student ability and interests, the difficulty of pupil adjustment should be lessened.

Team teaching is more than a simple manipulation of time and people; planning begins with the most feasible means by which students can learn what is to be taught, and then other factors are organized accordingly.

Consultants

Consultants can be valuable in helping start a team teaching program, so helpful, in fact, that any large scale program for innovating team teaching needs the services of qualified outside specialists. These should be selected for their ability to help teachers acquire the necessary knowledge and skills for changing to team teaching. Consultants used should have a background of successful experience with the operational phases of team teaching. One caution about consultants: they can be helpful only if carefully selected and asked to advise within the field of their special competence. Few people would employ a plumber to do an electrician's work, but schools often retain consultants without regard to what they hope the consultants will accomplish. It is little wonder that consultants occasionally fail to meet local expectations and that valuable time, money and talent are needlessly expended.

The program for inaugurating team teaching should not only anticipate many of the more difficult adjustments in adapting personnel, procedures and facilities to team teaching, but it should build the concepts upon which the new instructional approach will be based.

Some Suggestions for Implementation

Teachers and administrators generally have a genuine desire to provide the best instructional program possible within their capabilities. Parents also have an obvious vested interest in the quality of educational opportunity afforded their children. There are many techniques the implementor can use to channel this interest and desire for improved education toward the common goal of innovating team teaching.

Observing existing programs is probably the best single source of help available to a school preparing to implement team teaching. Most important of the numerous contributions visitation can make is the opportunity to obtain over-all perspective by observing team teaching programs in operation. Not only should different programs be seen, but alternative solutions to specific problems may be sought. The purpose of observation is not to copy other programs, but rather to explore the potential of a variety of approaches.

Specific checklists or questions should be prepared in advance of visitation. Written reports and critiques should be made following visitations. At all times evaluation of what is observed should have, as its frame of reference, application to the local school.

Key lay people and members of the board of education may be included in planning as well as in the actual visitation.

It is wise to visit a variety of team teaching programs, but emphasis should be on selecting a school whose approach most closely approximates the type of organization contemplated locally. The basic requirement in visitation is to know what to look for before the actual visit.

An added dividend of visitation is the enthusiasm generated after visiting a school that is deeply committed to, and effectively using, team teaching.

Limited special projects should be an integral part of any preparation for team teaching. For example, experimentation, even in a limited form, provides staff experience and encourages innovation. Additionally, experimentation has a local demonstration potential that can be profitably exploited. Increasing the scope of such experimental projects is a form of implementation in itself.

The term *research* always becomes involved in any discussion of projects and experimentation. It is most important to clearly define the purpose of research when speaking within the context of implementation, for there are certain requirements of true research which may not serve any useful purpose for implementation. If the project is true research, a rigid design must be developed, exacting procedures must be carefully followed and proper statistical treatment applied. Needless to say, most schools are ill equipped to handle such an undertaking, probably because it is felt that energy spent in keeping a detailed account of what is happening can be better spent on improving the program.

Another type of experimentation that has become popular within recent years is action research. This may have more practical value for the local school than true research. Flexible procedures are used for establishing the research design, but the purpose of implementation may be better served by this type of activity. For example, rather than constructing an elaborate design, students and teachers may be asked to render a value judgment reaction to the two forms of teaching, conventional and team. Periodic data gathering based on such value judgments can be most helpful in developing educated guesses concerning team teaching in both its implementative and operational stages. Opinionnaire is the term sometimes given such data-gathering instruments. These opinionnaires can give the administrator a clue as to what parts of the program need adjustment and improvement.

Workshops and Publications Have a Place

Probably the best in-service training device used is the workshop. An essential aim of this type of activity is to set aside a block of time for depth consideration of team teaching. The workshop buys time so teachers can work without the annoyance and distraction of other obligations, thus permitting total concentration on the subject.

Specific determination of purpose, delimitation of topic, tight organization, use of qualified experts as consultants and adequate time are keys to a worthwhile workshop. For example, a one-day workshop on the general topic of team teaching will be of questionable assistance in that no realistic consideration on a topic of this magnitude can be made within the time limitation.

The summer workshop held for a number of weeks is most desirable in that it provides an ideal setting for the innovator to blend the ingredients of change with staff members working together in close proximity. Such an experience contributes directly toward team unity. With the extensive exchange of ideas and group interaction, team members can be intellectually stimulated, particularly if new insights are contributed by consultants to enhance the scope of study and exploration.

Few instructional staffs have sufficient internal resources to give the extended workshop its needed perspective in the study of team teaching. If the innovation of team teaching is accorded sufficient commitment, funds for workshops should receive first priority.

Distribution of printed matter is a direct means of widespread community contact. Community understanding of team teaching can be approached through the preparation and widespread distribution of publications describing the new program. To be read, these materials must compete with professionally prepared publications; therefore, they must be artistically attractive and easy to read.

Pamphlets for general lay consumption are often the outgrowth of summer workshops. Two such examples are the *El Dorado Plan* prepared by the El Dorado, Arkansas, Public Schools and *Forecast for the Future*, a report of the Lakeview High School Plan in Decatur, Illinois. The specific purpose of these publications is to describe to the public the team teaching program being developed in the local high school. Each is less than twenty pages in length with an abundance of illustrations and diagrams. Each can be easily read in a few minutes, and either covers the essentials of the proposed programs.

A type of publication often prepared for internal use is a comprehensive definition of the proposed program. This includes the philosophy, goals, learning theory, procedures, organization and evaluative techniques of the program. Such a booklet is designed primarily for use within the profession; therefore, technical language and detailed treatment of the entire program can be used. During the pre-implementation stage the staff develops this statement. Often, it is sent to experienced educators for their evaluation and suggestion.

Periodic reports are valuable in keeping interested parties informed of progress. These may be in the form of reporting special projects, publicizing findings of opinionnaires and press releases. The local newspaper is a valuable source of community communication. Administrators will do well to use the newspaper often as a means of letting patrons know about team teaching progress.

Additional techniques that can be built into the implementation program are encouragement toward extensive reading of journals, demonstrations in faculty meetings, presentations by outside speakers and convention attendance.

Gradualism

No program for innovation can realistically proceed faster than the ability of the people involved to absorb the change. However, the design for change should be paced at the rate of the maximum capacity to adapt. Timetables for progress and long-range projections are necessary components of any well-organized plan, but progress must be basically dictated by the speed with which the people involved can change to the new program.

Change in educational programs should be approached from an evolutionary rather than a revolutionary perspective. Revolutions create immediate change, to be sure, but with damaging side effects in terms of shattered security and frustration.

The temptation to create a revolution in education has caused some schools to over-sing the praises of their programs. In an effort to arm themselves with sufficient tangible evidence to convince and impress their colleagues, they evaluate and judge team teaching programs before their "product" is thoroughly tested and proven. Truly, sequence and pace of innovation require the utmost precision in planning— and such is not always compatible wtih revolutionary change.

Attaching the label of evolutionary to change might be viewed by some as an opportunity to forestall any real innovation or as an excuse for lack of progress. To the contrary, although the suggested pace is less rapid, evolutionary change requires a carefully pre-determined design with definite sequence, pace and substance. These considerations are necessary to insure that purpose is always centrally focused and progress accomplished with all deliberate haste.

CHAPTER 7

Evaluation Considerations
for Team Teaching

by

JAMES L. OLIVERO

*Extensive study of curriculum programs and various pilot
studies in flexible scheduling, small group instruction, data
processing and evaluation of school programs marked
James Olivero's career as a school administrator.*

*As Research Assistant and Coordinator of the Stanford
University Intern Program, Mr. Olivero has worked in
close association with Stanford's Secondary Education
Project. Prior to his work in California, James Olivero was
assistant principal of Lakeview High School, Decatur,
Illinois. In his administrative capacity at Lakeview, Mr.
Olivero was a first-hand observer of a full-scale team
teaching project. He understands the procedures and
problems of team teaching, and is well qualified to evaluate the concept and its effects on today's schools.*

THERE's a joke of long standing that depicts a former high school
principal who moves into the halls of ivy and turns his attentions to
research. In his former position he would reply to the question, "How's
your wife?" in his usual amiable manner. As a professor, however, he
is likely to respond to the same question with a question of his own:
"As compared to what?"

Those who would advocate a shift to the team teaching system
have unfortunately been answering the question, "How's team teaching?" pleasantly and amiably, in the manner of the high school principal whose views are more affected by public relations than by academic considerations. Any objective evaluation of the system, how-

ever, must necessarily be approached from the viewpoint, "As compared to what?"

Advocates of team teaching are not alone in their folly. In professional literature there is little evidence of the subject, either pro or con, that can be substantiated by carefully controlled research results. Instead, the literature is replete with articles written by proponents of team teaching who subjectively discuss the merits of the device and articles written by opponents who, equally subjectively, expose the weaknesses of the device. Such hearsay makes provocative reading but offers little hope of an ultimate solution, for the authors of these articles ignore the basic question, the question that must be answered before any meaningful consideration is possible—"Team teaching compared to what?" Team teaching compared to the instruction which originally existed in our schools? Team teaching compared to education in some "ideal" school? Team teaching compared to some foreign educational systems (as some public school critics suggest)?

But even these questions must be begged temporarily. They must be begged because it is impossible to consider them until the basic terms have been defined; and nearly everyone has avoided definition.

Saying that team teaching is good or bad is like saying that liquid is good or bad. Unless the specific kind of liquid is identified, there is no possibility of arguing the question either way. When someone says team teaching is good or bad, we must know what particular application of it he is talking about. Until his terms are defined, he is talking nonsense. In all fairness, it must be said that writers and analysts are not the source of this haziness about team teaching. They have contributed to it, certainly, but the ambiguities, the diffusions of the concept, began elsewhere. They began with school administrators.

Following the advent of Sputnik, some schools adopted team teaching in an attempt to point out to their communities and to themselves that they were forward-thinking, that they were providing the kind of quality education which the people supplying the tax dollar demanded. Principals wore the banner of team teaching as if it were a symbol to the unknowing that their schools were progressive in the best sense of the word. A look at these schools quickly reveals the ambiguities that have arisen. In some schools the large groups range from 100 to 150 and the "small" groups enlist some thirty to forty students. Are these really small groups? Are these schools really accomplishing that which they set out to accomplish? Are they providing a program which provides quality education? Are these schools practicing team teaching or are they "playing the game"? These same questions can be raised in schools which may have the same-sized large groups, but that have scheduled their students so the small groups include no more than twelve to fifteen students. Are the answers any different for these schools than for those mentioned earlier?

So we arrive inevitably at an answer that, for the moment, must be assumed: Team teaching is any number of different kinds of programs, and though they bear certain common characteristics, they are each different too. It is a difficult concept, because of its inexactness, with which to begin assessment. But since it is all we have, it is the one we are forced to use.

That assessment is necessary goes without saying. Assessment is paramount. We must assess every inch of our snail-like progress if we are to determine the effectiveness of instructional programs. And the assessment must be designed so that evaluation becomes the key to improvement. But all assessment and evaluation must be carried out with the thought in mind that the thing we want to assess here is not exact, and we must be forever asking, "What are we comparing our results against? What is the measure of success?"

Let's make some assumptions about team teaching in a particular school. Let's assume that we are in a school which has teams composed of three members, that the large group meets twice per week for a module of thirty minutes, that the small groups are composed of twelve to fifteen students for two modules of time totaling sixty minutes and that adequate instructional resources are available. We must grant that these assumptions are categorically general, but using the assumptions as a base for reference, what relevant questions can we ask that will help us determine the effectiveness of our educational system?

We might ask the following questions:

THE TEACHING TEAM

1. Can teachers operate more effectively as individuals or in teams?
2. Can personality conflicts be avoided?
3. Can clerical assistance be utilized effectively?
4. Can teachers plan their time so they will be able to make additional preparations for improved instruction?
5. Can *esprit de corps* be developed among members of the team?
6. Can teachers assume specialized function responsibility?

Large Student Groups

1. Can lectures be presented in a dynamic, meaningful manner?
2. Can large groups be as effective with 200 students as they can with 50 students?
3. Can facilities be arranged to provide optimal visual and auditory accommodations?
4. Can needless repetition of material be avoided?
5. Can students be motivated in large groups?

Small Student Groups

1. Can teachers conduct small groups effectively?
2. Can teachers identify "power and prestige" figures in the small groups?
3. Can students profit from an opportunity of verbalizing concepts?
4. Can values be changed in small groups?
5. Can students interact with each other?
6. Can teachers in small groups do a more effective job of identifying in solving individual learning problems?

Student Instruction

1. Can students score better on achievement tests?
2. Can students retain and transfer generalizations, principles and concepts more effectively?
3. Can students adjust to a schedule which varies from day to day?
4. Can students receive individualized instruction?
5. Can creative learning experiences be provided?
6. Can students be taught individual responsibility for learning?
7. Can students of all ability profit from such an organizational structure?

Other Considerations

Human Resources:

1. Can non-school resource people be more effectively utilized?
2. Can the costs in terms of human energy and time balance out the advantages?
3. Can the drop-out rate be reduced?

Financial Resources:

1. Can materials be used more economically?
2. Can the per pupil cost of education be reduced?

Although these considerations have been listed as questions, they can be interpreted as hypotheses which need to be tested; for example, we hypothesize that teachers can operate more effectively in teams than as individuals. Naturally, this hypothesis needs to be more adequately defined. For instance, what do we mean by "effective"? Do we mean that teachers can learn to get along with one another or do we mean that students will receive improved instruction because of the cooperative planning in which the teachers have engaged? We may have various meanings; however, if comparisons are to be made, we need to define what we are comparing—more effective compared to what?

In the majority of cases, we will compare our hypotheses with the program which is currently practiced in our schools. Most schools which have attempted team teaching have approached the new experience in a piecemeal manner. Rather than jumping into the pool at the deep end and going "all-or-nothing-at-all," most schools have attempted team teaching on a trial basis in one or two departmental areas. English and/or social studies have been the departmental areas which have consistently "volunteered" to test the temperature of the water at the shallow end of the pool.

Perhaps the most unfortunate aspect of this approach has been the oversight of not establishing a control group with which comparisons can be made. The schools rationalize that the other departments and the classes therein act as the control groups. This is far from the case, however. Students in other areas are working with different curricular materials, are involved with different teachers, may be grouped differently and so on. Even the unsophisticated research person can recognize the inherent evaluative difficulties in this type of arrangement.

In schools organized to permit team teaching (and large and small groups), the lecture-discussion question is not one which can be considered from an either-or point of view since the organizational structure encourages a combination of lectures and discussions. What evidence is available to suggest the effectiveness of such an arrangement as this? A 1958 study found that students at New York University preferred a combination of lecture-discussion as opposed to either lecture or discussion. A similar study conducted at the State University of Iowa arrived at the same results as those found in New York.

As one reviews the literature to determine what has been done at the high school level, he is bombarded by descriptive but uncontrolled analyses of team teaching.

Far too few of the many high schools incorporating team teaching have attempted the practical evaluation of their programs, though at least five schools give some indication of systematic appraisal. The public schools in Jefferson County, Colorado, have conducted the most systematic appraisal of their team teaching innovations and other imaginative approaches. Three Illinois high schools—Ridgewood High School in Norridge, Lakeview High School in Decatur and Evanston Township High School in Evanston—have empirically tested hypotheses which they have established.

Dr. Scott Thompson, vice-principal at Homestead High School in Sunnyvale, California, recently completed a doctoral study in which he measured the retention of facts and generalizations in an experimental group (team taught) and a control group (taught in the traditional one teacher per thirty student class structure). His findings indicate that the students in the control group, tested immediately upon completion of the unit, scored significantly higher than the experimental group; however, when the two groups were tested twenty days later, the students in the experimental group gave evidence of retaining significantly more facts and generalizations than the students in the control group. The opportunity for students in small groups to express their opinions about facts and generalizations seems to have some effect on how well students retain the facts and understand the generalizations. Similar earlier experiments at Ridgewood, Evanston, Jefferson County and Decatur provide practically identical data.

All these schools were able to evaluate their programs because they knew what they were trying to find and set up the necessary procedures to accomplish their purposes.

Restrictions in Evaluation

Earlier we alluded to the fact that one of the reasons schools have a difficult time evaluating the effectiveness of their team teaching practices is because the schools are not certain what kinds of comparisons they are attempting to make. Assuming schools know what they are evaluating, what other restrictions have prevented systematic investigation?

Some administrators do not know how to set up controlled studies and, more unfortunate, they don't know where to go to receive the necessary help for setting up studies. Colleges and universities throughout the country should be supplying assistance to the schools, assistance which would help the schools determine the variables which must be controlled, explored and interpreted. Marshall High School in Portland, Oregon, and Lincoln High School in Stockton, California, have carefully prepared themselves for team teaching. They have built into the educational mechanisms of their programs evaluation procedures. They have turned to Stanford University for consultant services and for assistance in preparing for the kinds of evaluative data they wish to analyze.

Unfortunately, many school administrators have talked with professors in the schools of education who are not interested in the events transpiring in the high school and, therefore, provide little if any assistance to the schools. The cry for a cooperative agreement between the high schools and our schools of education is becoming more and more noticeable as we move away from some of the lockstep practices which we have been rehearsing for a hundred years. If the administrator in the school is a neophyte as far as sophisticated research is concerned, he is likely to steer away from tasks which will cause him difficulty.

If the administrator does not arrange for evaluation, who does? In most schools there is no single person other than the administrator charged with the responsibility of evaluation. With his many duties related to budgets, buses and books, it is little wonder that his evaluation turns to such global questions as, "Well, how did things seem to work out this past year?" This superficial question calls for superficial responses and the superficial responses will provide superficial evaluations.

It is a truism that the controls necessary in most research designs are difficult to manage within the practical setting of the school. For example, a high school in the Midwest was considering a cooperative venture with the research staff at a state university located near the high school campus. The university staff outlined the research proposal and detailed the approaches to be used for gathering data. In order to avoid a set on the part of staff and students, the university suggested that no mention be made to the teachers and the pupils about the team teaching structure prior to the opening of school. The logic of the university reasoning was sound; quite likely students and members of the faculty would have had a set toward team teaching. From a practical operating point of view, however, to have opened school without adequate student orientation, without a summer workshop during which teachers could study curricular offerings and make appropriate adjustments, and without informing the members of the community about the ensuing conditions, would have been sheer administrative suicide. Plainly, a dichotomous situation existed. In a very real sense the data would be biased if the participants were warned, but it would be unrealistic to expect the school to open without the necessary pre-planning.

Situations like this cause friction between the university and the school. The problem is not irresolvable, but commonsense compromises must be made. The school must understand the problems which exist in the preparation of the research design and the university must understand the school's problems if the two institutions are to complement each other in their quest for evidence.

Setting Up the Research Design

Anyone who has conducted an extensive and up-to-date survey of the various research designs relevant to educational problems will see the need for any investigator to seek validity in his research, to strive for both internal and external validity.

Internal validity means the degree to which the experimental treatment actually makes any difference in the specific experimental outcome. External validity means the degree to which the results of the experimental treatment can be applied to practical situations within the operational system of the school. To date, a great deal of research has been conducted at the college level which is internally and externally valid; that is, the experimental treatments are providing knowledge about the hypotheses. And this knowledge, in the form of significant variables, can be practically applied to teaching methods. To what degree the external validity suggests applicability to the high-school level is a moot question. But, obviously, research designs which are strong in both internal and external validity are the designs which we seek.

One educational survey analyzed sixteen specific research designs which, at one time or another, could prove to be valuable for those involved in hypothesis testing. Special note should be made of the point that no single research design is able to produce 100 per cent internal and external validity. And naturally it is more difficult to obtain external validity than it is to obtain internal validity.

Four basic research designs are especially relevant for those interested in testing hypotheses related to team teaching. If the reader will refer to the questions raised earlier, he will find a research design among the following classifications that will work for each of them. We can refer to the four designs by applying the following descriptive classifications:

1. Treat—test design
2. Test—treat—test design
3. Random test—treat—test *versus* random test—test design
4. Random test—treatment test *versus* random test—test *versus* random treatment—test *versus* random test design.

Assuming R represents random sampling, Tr represents treatment, and T represents test, the designs would be represented by the following formulae:

1. Tr—T
2. T—Tr—T
3. RT—T—T
   RT—T
4. RT—Tr—T
   RT—T
   R—Tr—T
   R—T

Although the first two designs represent the approach which is most frequently used, they in fact fail to answer the question, "As compared to what?" The first two designs may actually be considered pre-experimental designs. That is, based upon the results gathered from the control arrangements established for meeting the criteria in designs one and two, the educator can prescribe conditions which meet the demands of designs number three and four. Designs three and four help answer the question, "As compared to what?" because conditions are prearranged which make it possible for the evaluator to compare various treatments as measured by various tests. The treatments he elects to use are determined by the hypotheses which he establishes. The data he collects and the tests he makes are determined by the hypotheses and the treatments given.

Measuring the Efficiency of Team Teaching

Even the most vocal opponents of team teaching admit the administrative efficiency that team teaching permits. Descriptive analysis after descriptive analysis has suggested the advantages of having a teacher present a lecture one time to 150 students rather than five times to thirty students, as is so often the case in traditional systems. If team teaching can utilize the staff and the facilities more effectively, is this a sufficient finding to warrant the change from what exists to team teaching?

The answer to this question is extremely complicated, but most educators seem to agree on at least this single point: Increased efficiency is not sufficient justification unless instruction is significantly improved.

Let's assume three possible alternatives: (1) students learn more, (2) students learn equally as well and (3) students learn less in a team teaching system. Evidence which would support alternative three would lead to the rejection of team teaching, evidence of alternative one would lead to the acceptance of team teaching, but what about alternative two? If students learn as well and administrative efficiency is improved, is this enough to warrant change?

Unfortunately, the evidence which has been gathered since 1957 provides little in the way of interpretative analysis. The data seldom answer questions related to *any* of the three alternatives. The January issues of the *Bulletin* of the National Association of Secondary School Principals contain as many as thirty articles which explain various staff utilization projects. A large number of the articles refer specifically to team teaching and its advantages. It is not surprising to note that most of the articles find reasons to praise team teaching; most of the studies reported deal with administration rather than achievement level.

Some schools have attempted to determine what effect team teaching has on their students' achievement, but the studies are so poorly designed that conclusions with any degree of external validity are difficult to find. For example, some schools attempted to determine the effectiveness of team teaching by comparing the progress of a given class with the progress of a class which had preceded the experimental group. Few schools attempted to establish control groups for comparative purposes. In some cases inappropriate samples were gathered. Alternative interpretations of data were ignored in other cases. In essence, then, the data became self-fulfilling hypotheses; that is, they were interpreted in such a way that the hypothesis was accepted with given conclusions although other interpretations of the data seemed possible.

If after conducting a carefully controlled experiment the evaluator found that on standardized achievement tests no significant differences were found between the scores of the students in the control group and the scores of the students in the experimental group, what would this suggest? Would it indicate that team teaching was ineffective? One can realize the importance of interpreting the results he obtains in an objective manner. Assuming no significant gains in achievement were recorded, what alternative hypotheses are possible? Although space does not permit a complete analysis of the problem, there are reasons to believe that standardized tests may not be sensitive enough to indicate significant differences on achievement scores. (Certainly, this is one hypothesis which should be tested.) Achievement tests may not be sensitive enough to provide an accurate evaluation of "everything" which transpires in large and small group instruction as opposed to the instruction which takes place in the comparative situation. For example, it is doubtful whether achievement tests really measure generalizations. If the mastery of generalizations is a goal for both the experimental and control groups, it is doubtful whether achievement tests will provide an answer to this question.

Some teachers who work with small groups suggest, as one objective, the importance of helping students learn how to communicate and to interact with their peers in the group. They further suggest that small groups provide students with more possibilities of interacting than do classes which enroll thirty students. Interaction is not, however, synonymous with achievement. Achievement tests cannot be used to measure quantity or quality of verbal and non-verbal interaction in the small groups. This suggests, then, that those interested in measuring the difference between achievement in control and experimental groups adequately define what is meant by achievement. The tests used depend upon that which is defined as achievement. Achievement tests *per se* pose at least one problem for those considering evaluation of team teaching: *Achievement tests may not measure that which the researcher defines as achievement.*

Although one may suggest that achievement tests do not measure that which is defined, it is possible that he will consider those things which are measured by achievement tests important elements in the totality of the students' achievement. Even though the investigator may accept the result that the experimental students have not scored significantly higher, he must also assess the results to determine whether they have scored significantly lower. If the scores prove to be equal or higher, he can then turn his attention to other more specific objectives.

Another major consideration which is frequently tested is attitude. Educators generally agree that a positive attitude is a necessary, but not necessarily a sufficient, criterion for learning. Thurstone and

Likert-type attitude scales are instruments which can be administered to the participants involved in team teaching to test attitude formation.

Attitude scales are probably the easiest test instruments to administer; however, it is possible that more variation may be found in the results provided by these instruments than results from some other types of instruments. Attitude surveys administered at various times during the course of the year may provide the investigator with more reliable data. These, according to Beggs,* are the surest guide lines to administrative action in a school.

Attitude scales are especially valuable because they can be administered to some who cannot be measured by any other acceptable means. It is possible to obtain attitude ratings for faculty members and students, and even more important, for parents and other members of the community. Most parents can be expected to respond to attitude surveys even though they probably would be a little more hesitant and surely more negligent in responding to other types of instruments.

Of the three major categories discussed—administrative efficiency, achievement and attitudes—it is possible that positive results could be obtained from tests designed to measure alternatives one and three while negative results could be obtained from the tests designed to measure the effectiveness of alternative two. How does one make a decision to allow or to eliminate team teaching?

The Decision to Go Ahead—A Must!

Each major categorical hypothesis is composed of numerous sub-hypotheses. The sub-hypotheses must be arranged in hierarchical order so that the total evaluation can be based upon the quality of the accepted hypotheses rather than upon the number of accepted hypotheses.

For example, two sub-hypotheses related to achievement might be that (1) teachers will receive additional salary, and (2) per-pupil cost of instruction will be reduced. If the evaluator found that teachers could receive additional salary (paraprofessionals were able to assume some of the clerical duties normally assigned to teachers while teachers assumed additional student contact responsibilities), but he also found that pupil cost rose because teachers needed additional technical equipment to help them work with more students, he

* Cf. Chapter 2.

must make a decision—a decision which weighs the value of each sub-hypothesis. After weighing carefully all of the elements in each major category against every other element, he can determine the magnitude of the strengths and/or weaknesses of each category.

When comparisons are made between elements within a given category, values may be assigned to each element indicating that it is equal to, greater, or less in value than the other elements with which it is compared. Assigning E the designation of an element, the comparative values of specific elements may be represented thusly:

$$E_1 = E_2 \qquad\qquad E_1 > E_2 \qquad\qquad E_1 < E_2$$

In some cases the evaluator may wish to compare two or more elements with another element. This comparison can be represented in the following manner:

$$E_1 = E_3 + E_4 + E_5$$
$$E_1 < E_3 + E_4 + E_5$$

Once the evaluator is able to determine the global value of a specific category, he is able to compare that category with all other categories—in our example, administrative efficiency, achievement and attitudes. Following the same procedures which he utilized to determine values of the elements within a category, the evaluator establishes a hierarchy and value system for the three major categories. Almost invariably the achievement category will receive first rating.

No matter what the singular or combined values of administrative efficiency or attitudes may be, most evaluators insist that achievement in the experimental group must be equal to or greater than achievement in the control group before any additional factors are considered. If achievement were delegated the position of prime importance, achievement would be considered before all other factors. Only after the category of achievement had been analyzed carefully would other considerations relating to attitudes and/or administrative efficiency be made.

The final decision, then, is based on the data which answer the question, "As compared to what?" If the values of one system are greater than the values of another system, assuming that the costs are similar, the system which contains the most values for the least costs will be selected. This concept, expressed algebraically, can be stated thusly:

$$S_1 = V_5 - C_2 = D_3$$
$$\text{as compared to}$$
$$S_2 = V_3 - C_2 = D_1$$

In the previous graphic presentation S_1 (system) is equal to V_5 (value definition worth 5 units) minus C_2 (cost definition worth 2 units) which leaves D_3 (difference unit of 3 units). If S_1 is compared to S_2 and the difference between the values and costs is D_3 and D_1 respectively, the evaluator would select S_1 as being the most promising system to meet the demands of the criteria he has established because the difference value represents a net gain of two value units.

Does team teaching when compared with the current instructional system provide a value difference greater than that which exists? This is the real question which must be answered, a question which has gone unanswered.

Team Teaching in Retrospect

Evaluation of what has been done in team teaching is practically impossible! From the early studies that were made, many descriptive comparisons have been drawn; tight research designs, however, are at a minimum. The fact that sophisticated research designs have not been as apparent as one might hope does not in itself condemn team teaching. What has not been done must be done.

Administrators who are interested in explaining the possibilities of team teaching could well spend their time reviewing the literature which has been put into print—not from the point of view of evaluation, but from the point of view of what has been attempted by other schools. Using the literature as a frame of reference, team teaching programs which attempt to solve specific problems can be developed for specific school systems.

The evaluation facet of the total picture of team teaching is as important as the implementation of the program itself. As an integral part of the program, evaluation needs to be given careful consideration. If those involved are relatively unsophisticated in developing designs for the purpose of testing hypotheses, they should carefully state the questions which they hope to answer and then turn to research specialists for assistance in developing the design. Some school districts have research specialists as members of the staff; other assistance may be obtained from educational research specialists at the college level. Whatever the source, the time and energy put into the development of the design are well worth the resulting interpretative data. The administrator who follows the guides suggested here will be able to answer the question, "As compared to what?"

CHAPTER 8

A Teacher Comments on Team Teaching

by

DAVID TOMCHEK

Who is better qualified to talk about team teaching than a teacher so engaged?

A graduate of the University of Wisconsin, David Tomchek first taught English at Monroe, Wisconsin, and then went to Barrington, Illinois, to take part in Barrington High School's initial team teaching project.

The ideas he presents here come from not only his own experiences in the last two years but also from his discussions on the subject with other team teachers.

LET ME say at the outset that I do not view team teaching as a phenomenon isolated from other educational procedures. Indeed, I intend to present team teaching as only a part, albeit a meaningful part, of an attitude toward education. Such a view is essential, for without it we shall end up not having seen the jolly green forest.

Team Teaching and Students

One of the most erroneous assumptions teachers are likely to make is that a group of 100 students is less manageable than a group of twenty-five. Indeed, team teachers have found the opposite to be true; a large group tends to be attentive and much less easily distracted. Of course attention, we know, is directly related to the appeal of the material being presented.

This is not to say that large groups may be indiscriminately created and expected to perform without specific direction. In preparing students for a venture with team teaching, there are some important details of which students must be aware. Basically, students must understand the purpose of team teaching. They should be allowed to consider its favorable aspects. At the same time they need to be made aware that a successful program *depends* on their cooperation, and that, as in any educational venture, their cooperation is essential.

Perhaps most vital for students in a team teaching program is the ability to take notes. A team teacher should check students' notes periodically so that large group sessions are not allowed to become periods of passivity. In addition to checking notes, teachers should occasionally prepare tests aimed at enabling a student to determine for himself his ability to follow and record the emphases of lectures.

The team teacher can profit from this carefully controlled note taking too, for he can, through inspection, discover tangible evidence of his effectiveness or ineffectiveness. After all, if a number of students have missed a point, one must ask why. Answers to such accumulations of whys are valuable in terms of curriculum changes and improvements in specific units.

Although checking notes is probably a necessity, the large group sessions, because of the emphasis on individual responsibility, help students toward independence. Ideally, in a carefully planned developmental program, students should eventually learn to evaluate lectures and indicate in small groups what information has not been adequately covered, and the checking of notes should theoretically become unnecessary. Again, lecture quizzes could continue to be a valuable source of evaluative information for teachers.

Team teachers have found that a certain amount of student independence comes about unexpectedly. In some units taught to a group of seventy-five junior English students in one school, the teachers were unable to provide texts for each of the students, so they set up a reserve book system in the library. Of course college students rapidly become oriented in the use of such systems, but the high school staff were a bit concerned at first because they knew their students were accustomed to having texts carefully placed in their hands. With the aid of the librarian, the reserve system was set up, and, much to the faculty's delight, the students unquestioningly adjusted to the new system.

As far as the team teaching staff were concerned, the success of the reserve book system raised the question of the value of the standard text so automatically issued to each student. Not only were the teachers in agreement as to the tedium and insipidness of most high school English texts, but they wanted to be able to include more material than was included in the standard texts. The reserve system accomplished this, and, more, pointed toward a broader concept and a broader application, because a reserve system need not be created for team teaching alone; there is no reason why such a system cannot service the entire school.

Teams and Administrators

Team teachers expect an administrator to encourage not only team teaching, but anything else in the way of innovation. That encouragement is the most vital contribution an administrator can make, especially when he is dealing with teachers who are specialists in their subject areas.

More important than the statement of support, however, is the demonstration of that attitude. We can find tangible evidence in what an administrator is willing to provide his team teachers in three areas.

Scheduling. Once plans are formulated, the administrator can be expected to schedule students so that the maximum goals of the team may be approached. For example, teachers participating on teams should have common planning periods. Ignoring this elementary aspect of convenient scheduling means setting up unnecessary difficulties. (It should be pointed out that the whole matter of scheduling is being discussed intensively in the professional literature.*)

Time. Innovation in education occurs so slowly because no one is willing to make time available for experimentation. In other words, if we are going to try new approaches, then teachers should have reassigned time during the working day, or teachers should be paid during a summer in which plans can be developed. The simple fact is that when teachers are teaching five hours a day, they barely have time and energy to produce, let alone create. To expect brilliant lectures in addition to the usual workaday chores is to expect the impossible. Experience has demonstrated the necessity of time to plan.

In one sporadic effort in one school, teams were used on both the junior and senior levels. Three teachers combined three classes, and two of them were participating on both teams. In addition to the classes they were teaming (as the expression goes), they were responsible for three other classes. The result of such a burden was in

---

* See *The Bulletin* of the National Association of the Secondary School Principals, May, 1963, and Beggs, D. W., *The Decatur-Lakeview Plan* (Prentice-Hall, 1964).

some cases inadequate preparation, and the natural result of that, we all know, is inadequate instruction. The resilience of youth can probably tolerate periods of poor teaching, but teachers cannot retain their interest and vigor in the face of frustrating inadequacies they cannot control.

Time for working, planning and thinking (now there's a queer possibility!) must be made available to the teacher. And if making time means spending money, as it most surely does, then the administrator must either gird himself for the onslaught or oil the PR mechanism.

Facilities. While it is totally and disgustingly true that where there's a will, there's a way, the acceptance of such ho-hummery represents much that is feeble in education. Granted that the people who innovate or labor under duress are to be praised, struggle does not necessarily enhance the flavor of success. Accordingly, facilities for team teaching should be made easily available so that teachers can concentrate on teaching rather than on locating PA's and overhead projectors. Ideally, the large group room will have a lecture deck which includes phonograph, tape recorder, overhead projector and public address system. In addition, the room should be equipped with blackout curtains for movie and slide viewing. The emphasis on equipment is not the result of an obsession with gadgets, but comes rather from an awareness of the effectiveness of such equipment in dealing with large groups.

The administrator must be willing to provide funds for adequately supplied rooms. His reluctance to do so can cripple the best plans. Administrative support of educational programs means that these problems, mundane as they are, shall be solved by the administrator, whose job it is, after all, to facilitate the educational program.

A Plea to Administrators

The suggestion that an administrator's job is the facilitation of the educational program leads to the tender and nebulous question of the administrative role in general. It is difficult to remain *au courant* in administrative theory, but lately there has been a great emphasis on leadership, much of it the result of recent studies in leadership theory. Accordingly, there are frequent references to emerging leadership, charismatic leadership, dynamic leadership and the like. Too, a lively interest is being shown in the theory of roles and role expectations, as opposed to institutional and societal expectations. Followed to its logical extreme, the emphasis on leadership and roles can result only in increased facility in the manipulation not only of teachers, but of education as well.

Administrators, especially in a team teaching program, should start with one basic assumption. Teachers are hired to perform specific jobs for which they are specifically trained. An English teacher probably knows more about English education than his administrator. Accordingly, he would like to think that he is competent enough to determine how best he can perform his professional tasks. When he has an idea for improving his work, he expects encouragement on the part of administrators rather than demands for the justification of his ideas.

What has all this to do with team teaching? To reiterate, team teaching is not an isolated educational phenomenon, and it is almost certain that whoever first suggested team teaching—even before we had a neat alliterative phrase to identify it—was met with a demand for justification by someone who wanted to be a manipulator of men rather than a provider of facilities.

Besides offering moral support and dealing with the technicalities of schedule, time and facilities, the administrator should also consider the possibility that failure means little more than success. However, in terms of educational goals, success and failure are equally valuable. On the surface this appears paradoxical, but a moment's thought can provide a bit of wisdom. Every time we fail, we provide ourselves with a fact that some procedure or idea did not work under some particular circumstances. If one fails in trying to teach reading by empathy, he learns something nearly as valuable as he would have learned through success. He is then ready to try something else.

Many teachers, and not only team teachers, have had ideas dismissed because educators (including department heads who perform administratively, depending on the vagaries of peculiar bureaucracies) have a fear of failure. The rejection speech goes something like this, "Our Mr. S. tried a similar idea back in 1953, or was it '54? Well, anyway, it was the year we had the bad trout season. Couldn't get a decent fish to save your soul. Anyway, he tried it, and the kids didn't seem to take to it so well."

In fact, all the Mr. S's learned only one thing: they as individuals could not make the idea work.

All this leads gracefully to the matter of what constitutes a good idea successfully made operational. Mr. S. may have had a tremendous idea, but his personal abilities, or a lack of support, or any of countless other factors, may have prevented the idea from becoming a successful program. Neither success nor failure in education is an absolute comment on the quality and possibility of an idea.

Applied specifically to team teaching, this philosophy means that the failure of a single attempt at team teaching does not prove the idea of the system is bad. On the contrary, the obvious and dramatic success some teachers have had proves that, under the right conditions, team teaching can be a superior educational program.

Give Us This Day Our Daily Thought

The question of success *versus* failure is made doubly complex by the tendency in education, as in social sciences generally, for practitioner and theoretician alike to assign causes with the mad glee of a Frankenstein. "All but one of the following," the objective question reads, "are *causes* for the growth of the labor movement." Or we are told that a child did not learn punctuation, "because he wasn't paying attention during class." And it is not unusual in professional literature for researchers to assign etiological significance on the basis of concomitant factors, a faulty technique which is covered in even the most elementary rhetoric books.

The result of a careless approach to questions of causality might be this kind of statement: "Since we started team teaching, the youngsters are more enthusiastic and seem to be learning more." Such remarks imply a causal relationship where one may not be clearly established. This is especially so if consideration is given to the Hawthorne Effect, which indicates that mere attention seems to affect productivity in the factory.

Another example of carelessness in linking cause and effect is the teacher who claims superiority for drill methods *because* she teaches punctuation by drill methods and all her children certainly know their punctuation. The question is all too obvious. Might not they have learned as quickly and as well by some other method? Alas, we can never experiment with her particular students because they already know punctuation.

Fallacious determination of causes may encourage teachers and administrators to venture into team approaches, and this would only be natural in view of the popularization of team teaching in both professional and popular periodicals. Too often sketchy articles which discuss successful educational programs imply that team teaching is causally related to a favorable outcome. Because team teaching is likely to be the newest and most touted of any particular school's method, the observer sees the obvious and misses other qualities which may be present and perhaps more influential.

Then there is the popularity of the method. Once team teaching became identified in the popular mind as *the* innovation, the via-Luce intellectual began inquiring on parents' night if his son's high school was team teaching. The situation is comparable to what occurred after Conant recommended that every student be required to write a theme a week, provoking such parental questions as, "Why don't you have the kids write more?" Some teachers no doubt wanted to answer that they disagreed with the recommendation, but that verged on heresy and un-Americanism. Instead, we relied on the defense that invariably we were teaching more than a hundred students and were finding a theme a week excessive.

At present the parental inquiries about team teaching are increasing, and we are confronted with a situation in which, in order to seem good, we must follow the trend. Administrators, faced with an anxious, semi-informed populace, may be panicked into sudden change. If so, they will bring on the deadly decline that is fostered by ill-informed and hasty planning. If team teaching ultimately fails, it may well be due to the abuses caused by fadism.

Teams and Teachers, or "Pass the Hemlock, Please"

Someone observed that the panacea for the crisis in education was a Socrates in every classroom. A friend shrewdly wondered, "Will there be enough hemlock to go around?" This frivolity involves part of the team teaching issue because it raises a vital question, one which teachers admit privately but unfortunately ignore publicly. That question is whether or not all teachers are equally endowed intellectually and practically.

The tradition-bound teacher tends to believe that anyone who holds a degree must surely be able to convey information to any child. Reduced to the ridiculous, this means, "I know how to add 2 plus 2; therefore, I can teach this skill." And in some subject areas an additional folly is perpetrated: "I am an English major; therefore, I can teach literature, composition, grammar, English history, art appreciation, research skills, social poise and democracy-in-case-nobody-else-is-doing-it." The point is that teachers cannot be all things to all people. Team teaching helps teachers narrow the focus of their efforts so that emphasis is placed on areas in which they are most prepared and competent.

Most teachers are most satisfied when they have an opportunity to function to their fullest capacity in the field of their greatest preparation, which is also presumably their field of greatest interest. In other words, we teach best what we enjoy most.

We sometimes hear history teachers saying, "Well, I just couldn't get through the Reconstruction this year." Obviously not, if the teacher has a thing about the Civil War. All of which leads to that same ugly question—a question vital to team teachers—of quantity *versus* quality. Can't a sense of history be learned through emphasizing a single period rather than racing breathlessly through the centuries? Can't a year profitably spent in the study of the novel produce as much a sense and/or appreciation of literature as a year meticulously divided among other literary forms? The answers to such questions are as varied as the so-called objectives of such courses, and the important consideration here is the milieu in which the statement of objectives occurs.

Normally, teachers like to think that they are essential as objective staters, and the feeling is shared by administrators and school boards and their constituencies as well. If we were able to follow an objective from its genesis to its final corpulent statement in a mimeographed curriculum guide, we would probably be astounded, for most of us are hopelessly tangled in a skein of pettiness and pride.

In discussing innovation and its relationship to administrators, we indicated the need to beware of the ear-to-the-public educator who innovated largely as his employers desired. While some administrators may leap too eagerly at the opportunity to innovate, there are others, largely teachers, who view change as a threat to proven procedures. Some conservatives, I'm sure, act out of conviction and deliberation, and it would be unfair to question their integrity. On the other hand, we would be blind if we ignored the number of conservatives who selfishly uphold the traditional because they have teaching down to a pattern.

For example, during the third week of the second semester, the unit on Shakespeare is dragged out ("It seems to go over better in winter!"), and the faded lettering announces, "Shakespeare: His Life, His Times, His Plays," and the drab pictures present a variety of scenes from a particular play. The machinery is now in motion for the production of sugar-cube and/or balsa wood models of the Globe Theatre, colored maps of Shakespeare's London, tiresome, ratty-haired, doll-like representations of the characters and genealogical tables of anybody remotely connected to the play or the Elizabethan era. There are faded and carefully guarded dittoed quizzes on each act, and the unit is concluded with a five-page, multiple-choice, true-false, fill-in-the-blanks examination. Teachers are not alone to blame for such hackneyed approaches. A major portion of the responsibility must, of necessity, be divided between educators and the public they serve rather than educate.

Team teaching helps insure that planning and evaluation will be continuous and dynamic. Fresh approaches to content become the rule rather than the exception.

The Business of Teaming

Hasn't every teacher reached a point of fatigue as he goes through a presentation for the fourth or fifth time in a day? Out of all that fatigue grew the idea of somehow eliminating the repetition. Some teachers just plain grew sick of saying late in the day, "Now, as I told you— or did I tell you? Did I say that yesterday to this class? Hmm. Well . . ."

Some of the answers to the problem were really obvious. No teacher, for example, should teach more than two identical courses. Another solution was to provide the individual teacher with a time or times in which he could provide instruction for the entire group for which he was responsible. A third possibility was a renewed emphasis on elaborate and carefully prepared lesson plans. And a fourth solution was team teaching, a method whereby two or more teachers combined their classes and their resources as teachers.

Of these possibilities team teaching has received the greatest emphasis and recognition both professionally and popularly, and justifiably so, for team teaching does a great deal more than simply offset repetition and boredom.

One teacher, in evaluating her first experience with team teaching, commented that a new and real pressure to excel came from the fact that she was not only providing instruction for students but for teachers as well, because as she lectured the members of the team sat listening. The result of such an audience provided the teacher with incentive to teach, to go beyond a presentation off the top of her head.

The team approach has the unique advantage of allowing participants to teach in the area of their interests. This amounts to specialization, yet the team approach does not negate the requirement that all members be well-rounded and participate in small group discussions and in the planning and evaluation of a unit. Specialization is a danger only when it occurs at the expense of broad interests, and that fortunately is not necessarily the case among team teachers.

Equally as important as specific interests are specific abilities. There are teachers who don't care to discuss an idea or fact calmly with students. They are the people about whom students say, "We just can't say anything at all!" Fine. In a team teaching system such people can be utilized as lecturers. On the other hand, there are teachers who prefer the intimacy of personal acquaintance. They can direct the discussion groups. Depending on the type of team organization, teachers may be allowed to perform the duties for which they are most suited.

The kind of team should be carefully considered, of course, before a team program is implemented. Essentially, there are two kinds of teams. One is the hierarchical type, in which a master teacher performs quasi-administratively for a group of teachers. At the same time these masters are expected to be particularly skilled in their teaching areas. This concept is based on the idea that groups, in order to perform effectively, must have clearly defined leadership which is never inhibiting but always encouraging. The advantages of a hierarchy are obvious: Decisions can be made, responsibility can be assumed, direction can be provided, duties can be clarified.

Besides the hierarchical method, there is the cooperative system in which a leader is not designated, and in which decisions are the result of interaction and discussion. In terms of increased effectiveness, as opposed to efficiency, the cooperation method has much to offer. If the members of such a team are ruled by candor, there is every possibility that the result of their interaction will be an increased awareness of themselves, as they relate to instruction. Ideally, members should be able to say that a particular presentation was badly organized. If a teacher is unable to take, or give, such abrupt criticism, then he probably should not participate in such intensive interactions.

Another important need of the cooperative team member is the ability to submit finally to the wishes of the majority even when individually he may disagree or disapprove. After a year of cooperative effort, one teacher said bluntly that he would never do it again. And the reason was simply that he had to be able to control the entire program. He was neither interested in nor able to participate effectively in units with which he did not wholeheartedly concur. On the other hand, another member of the same team said the scrutiny of his peers and their frank evaluations provided for so much growth that he had become an ardent advocate of the cooperative method. Obviously, these are purely individual matters and difficult to evaluate impartially.

To return then to the matter of teachers performing in the areas of their greatest effectiveness, the hierarchical method is one in which responsibilities are more specified. For example, the master would not be expected to assume the full burden of small group discussion if he was obligated to provide the greatest share of large group instruction. Some variations on this plan propose a number of levels of authority descending from master to teacher to grader to clerk. In this way, it would be easier to assign responsibilities to the individuals.

The cooperative method, however, requires more of each individual, usually demanding that the teacher be adept in both small and large group work. In terms of teacher self-improvement, there is a distinct advantage here because peers can give and take criticism more freely than can authorities. A master is, after all, just that.

Myth Making

Occasionally, exaggerated claims are made for team teaching. Among such claims is the one that students learn more as a result of having been team taught. Drawing such conclusions is dangerous because the issues are obscured. The ultimate goal, naturally, in any educational innovation is the accomplishment of more. That is to say that if we were able, we would like to produce more Einsteins per capita at the same time that we help people become happier. At present there is no evidence to indicate that team-taught children have learned more or less than any other students. All we have are statements to the effect that the team approach solved specific problems. In one school, participating on a team provided new teachers with what was considered to be an improved orientation because of the close working relationships with experienced teachers. Other teachers report personal enthusiasm for the system, or what they think is improved learning.

Then there is the student inventory, a device prepared by educators in an attempt to eliminate the need for self-flattery. In these inventories we find such loaded questions as: "Do you think you derived increased benefit from team teaching? Has the study of biology become more meaningful?" More meaningful than what? The previous study of biology? Or perhaps more meaningful than the study of English? To expect students to make such judgments is an invitation to nonsense, for judgments must be made in the presence of stand-ards, and education persists as the most standardless institution in modern society. We don't know *what* people should learn, let alone *how* or *why.*

Perhaps the most distressing claim for team teaching is that it always provides more time for the teachers. It is perfectly true that while one member of a team is lecturing the others may be preparing their own units or correcting their own papers. But we've already said that one advantage of teaming is learning from other teachers, and this requires attending and paying attention to lectures, which quickly takes up the slack. One solution is to make the team so extensive that two or more lecture sessions must be given. Team members would attend only the first lecture, gaining time while the second or third lecture for the day was being given. During this free time teachers could work individually with students. However, time in which to work and create and think is never the result of a new process alone. Free time is the result of technological improvement, of additional staff or of reduced class responsibility. While the team approach may reduce some class responsibility, it increases the responsibility for class preparation so disproportionately that one is likely to hear, "I just don't have the time to teach well and still remain a human being." Excellence is the result of genius or effort, and teachers are generally too exhausted to exhibit the latter.

Deciding to Attempt

The final decision to team teach is obviously a shared one, just as is the final decision to attempt anything in the way of innovation. In one case two teachers and their administrator decided to team a pair of English classes, but unfortunately the decision found little in the way of implementation. The large group room provided was an airless, badly illuminated, shabbily furnished room in which the metal rafters added unpleasantly to the factory atmosphere. The students misbehaved, the teachers became irritated and haggard, the principal said something was wrong, and they all concluded that team teaching did not work. The point is that a decision is not an isolated moment in time and space. Just as it has its antecedents, so it will have its results, and the joint effort in education must be directed toward controlling, and thereby attempting to understand, the factors which shape the results. Accordingly, decisions must be implemented, facilities and time provided, performances evaluated.

Occasionally we hear that one of the functions of an administrator is to serve as the decision maker. This is probably true in light of two facts. First of all, the national meetings for administrators are well attended, and naturally so, for a school system can better afford to have its administrator inspired than its teachers. There are fewer of the former. Second, the professional journals available to administrators are far more innovation-minded than are the esoteric journals in the subject matter areas. Inasmuch as teachers tend to be unfamiliar with what's new, the administrator appears as the innovator. If teachers become aware of the sources of ideas, if they begin reading such periodicals as the *Bulletin* of the National Association of Secondary School Principals, and if they begin thinking of education rather than of how to teach English or music, then there will be a good possibility that innovation, and all of education with it, will become the shared responsibilities of teachers and administrators. This can occur if we begin having administrators whose preoccupation is education rather than administration, principals in the sense of "principal teacher," rather than of "manipulator of the public funds." The result could be interesting.

Doubting Around

Of all the disgusting misinterpretations to which we are constantly subjected, one of the most irritating is that surrounding the quality of confidence. Teachers are expected to exhibit confidence as well as every other well-adjusted, normal clean-living American. Unfortunately, confidence is too often interpreted as satisfaction. "I am confident that I am doing well, that I am teaching America's youth in the ways of truth and democracy," runs the cliché. If we are confident, we are tired and old, for the only confidence we can allow ourselves as teachers is the confidence that both we ourselves and our methods can improve.

In order to improve we must be willing to doubt ourselves and our abilities, and we must acquire the perspective in which we can doubt the value of the entire educational process and its relationship to modern society. To doubt is to question, and that means finding answers.

CHAPTER 9

An Administrator Looks at Team Teaching

by

FRANCIS M. TRUSTY

Having been teacher, vice-principal, principal and college professor, Francis M. Trusty has seen most aspects of team teaching. As principal of Glenbrook North High School at Northbrook, Illinois, for example, he assisted teams in academic and fine arts areas. As a professor he is concerned with introducing his students to the promises and pitfalls of team teaching.

Dr. Trusty has won many honors, such as a Stanford University Honors Scholarship and a Kellogg Foundation Internship. He has been chairman of the Oregon State T.E.P.S. Commission. He has written for the professional journals and has spoken before meetings of the American Association of School Administrators, the Stanford Cubberly Conference and others.

Presently Assistant Professor of Education, Department of Educational Administration, Rochester, New York, Dr. Trusty brings a theoretical orientation and practical experience to his consideration of team teaching.

ADMINISTRATORS must take a professional and realistic look at team teaching, carefully considering both the advantages and the drawbacks. For team teaching, or any sweeping change in school practice, will require an initial expenditure of administrative time and energy. At the outset, then, a school administrator needs to make a decision as to whether or not he wants to pay the price, regardless of the reward.

In some school districts, the building administrator is expected by the board of education and the central office administrators to take the direction of team teaching. In other districts, the principal's motivation is an idealism which leads him to believe that team teaching promises to be a better way for teachers to teach and, thus, for students to learn.

The weight of the balance in favor of team teaching will be determined largely by the administrator's ability to motivate the teaching staff to adopt the concept. If administrators are surrounded, often as a result of their own employment practices, by experimentally minded teachers, the decision to team teach becomes easy to finalize and not too difficult to implement. This does not imply that team teaching cannot be implemented in a traditionally oriented school.

The administrator who believes the school's job is simply to select and transmit facts will feel no compulsion to use team teaching for this kind of instruction. Intellectual achievement, he reasons, is the result of self-discipline, not of modified teaching techniques. The administrator who believes it is the responsibility of the school to motivate and develop each student's total understanding of the world in which he lives may welcome team teaching as a new approach to this age-old problem. Administrators of school systems able to compete financially for an outstanding teacher in every classroom may feel no need for a teacher to specialize, as is often required in team teaching. Such administrators reason that their staff is equally good at all phases of instruction. However, if attracting well-qualified teachers is a problem, the administrator needs to explore every avenue for better utilizing what few superior teachers he may have.

The capable administrator sensibly considers each factor operating in his school system and community before making a decision to inaugurate team teaching. To do less than this is to invite failure of the project.

Among the administrator's considerations as he studies the potential of team teaching are the boundaries within which he must operate. Is the present quality of instruction satisfactory or can it be improved? Would team teaching be apt to meet with favorable reaction from parents and school board members? What material and facility resources can be made available to the project? Are the limitations imposed by state and regional accreditation agencies too restrictive to sanction team teaching? How will teacher load be affected? What kind of help is available to resolve the scheduling problems?

Not least among the administrator's thoughts are those having to do with control of the educational program and the direction that control is to take. He will want to know how he can exercise control in a system where administrative responsibility is decentralized. He will consider whether the existing channels of communication will function adequately. He needs to know who will make decisions about content. He must know who coordinates, administers and provides over-all supervision of the teams. The administrator, finally, must know what kind of in-service education will be required to prepare teachers for team teaching assignments.

Every administrator is concerned about maintaining or promoting a professionally respectable image of his school. Thus, the quality of instruction becomes important as a means of determining the community's attitude toward the school. Team teaching should contribute a favorable image to this attitude.

The vested interests of faculty members and administrators in preserving their positions, maintaining their roles and exercising influence, tend to promote a sense of balance between the past and any current idea of wholesale change.

And so, the administrator reasons, who else but the foolhardy, the brash and unknowing young neophyte, or the extremely mature veteran would seriously dare to suggest wholesale change? Team teaching, he thinks, may be difficult to sell to the faculty, to board members and to parents. Would it not be easier to justify greater expenditures of money to improve the present system than to introduce a change, particularly when no one can be sure that team teaching will be better than the tried and true methods? And how can the administrator provide satisfactory assurances to everyone that team teaching will be any better or that what has worked elsewhere will be successful here?

The administrator's feelings notwithstanding, however, team teaching as a new approach is being tried in almost every state. Professional publications have carried the story of successful team teaching projects to all corners of the land. What about the failures? Perhaps they, like old soldiers who never die, just faded away.

Every administrator knows that the quality of instruction in his school can be improved, that some of the public criticism is justified and that team teaching does offer an alternate course of action. But there are other courses of action for bringing about increased quality in the schools. Team teaching should be considered as one, not the only alternate. But if he decides in favor of team teaching, the administrator's interest in team teaching will be primarily related to its potential for fulfilling local expectation of improving the educational opportunities available.

Boundaries Within Which the Administrator Must Function

Boundaries constitute limitations within which an administrator must function. For the most part, such boundaries serve to restrict the choices available to the administrator. They tend to make compromise an integral part of his decision making process. They limit the distance he can go in any one direction. Such limitations are an integral part of the balance-preserving machinery. Specific areas of possible limitations are discussed below.

QUALITY OF INSTRUCTION

To each person "quality instruction" has a different meaning. To students it may mean more individual help from the teacher; to the teacher it may mean students who are more enthusiastic about what the teacher is teaching. To some parents higher grades for their children are evidence of quality instruction. To some administrators higher scores on standardized achievement tests and more students accepted at better colleges are evidence of quality instruction. Other administrators consider a low dropout rate as evidence of quality instruction. In any event, a pledge that team teaching will improve the quality of instruction is to suggest that a panacea has been found.

But only as the phrase "quality of instruction" is carefully interpreted in terms of improved retention of subject matter knowledge, a better understanding of material discussed, a greater skill in ability to use concepts presented or other specified objectives, will it be possible to pledge an improvement in the quality of instruction and, thereby, fulfill any expectation for team teaching.

AVAILABILITY OF FINANCIAL SUPPORT

In its early stages, team teaching, along with educational television, school district reorganization and programmed learning, was grasped on the basis that it would save money. Such is not the case. Improvement of instruction results from human endeavors involving a greater expenditure of time, energy and effort. Such endeavors usually require a greater expenditure of money rather than less. Additional specialized resources, such as overhead projectors, large screens, transparencies and sound systems require more, not less money. For the administrator with more needs than money, this poses a problem.

At Glenbrook North High School in Northbrook, Illinois, one large lecture room for 125 students has been equipped with a sound system, darkening facilities, overhead projector and a large screen at a cost of $1,300. The installation of movable partitions to divide one large lecture room into six normal-sized classrooms at Glenbrook South High School resulted in a cost of $30,000 beyond what it would have cost to install cement block walls. One agency that has undertaken to study economical ways and means of modifying existing structures to accommodate team teaching is the Educational Facilities Laboratory.*

FUNCTION OF ACCREDITATION AGENCIES

At the beginning of each school year, a package of forms arrives in the administrative office. Each form must be returned within a given period of time. The answers provided to the questions asked determine whether the school will again be accredited by the state or the regional accrediting association. Full credit courses must meet for 200 minutes per week; laboratory classes must meet for 275 minutes per week. A teacher must not teach more than six periods daily on the lengthened period schedule. Academic teachers may not teach more than 170 students per day. Deviation from the standards must have approval.†

While the limitations imposed upon the school by accreditation agencies are by and large not prohibitive, they do constitute a restriction making for inflexibility. Team teaching, by contrast, is an attempt to introduce greater flexibility into the instructional program.

NATURE OF HUMAN RELATIONSHIPS

In any school there is a complex structure of human relationships. Secretaries, custodians, teachers, department chairmen, administrators and board members are all a part of this structure. The formal structure consists of positions—the hierarchical location of any person within the structure; and roles—the manner in which the person performs his job. The informal structure is much less readily identified but exerts considerable influence through its members who hold positions in the formal structure.

Any administrator attempting to inaugurate team teaching must

* Educational Facilities Laboratories, Inc., 477 Madison Ave., New York, N.Y.
† Taken from the *Policies and Criteria for the Approach of Secondary Schools*, statement of the North Central Association of Colleges and Secondary Schools.

be cognizant of these relationships within his school if the project is to be successful. If new positions are to be created, the way they fit into the formal hierarchy must be determined.

EQUALITY OF TEACHER LOAD

The school policy on teacher load is an area of interest to teacher applicants. The policy varies from district to district but tends to be uniform within a district. Five classes plus a study hall and a division room assignment is compared by the applicant to, "... it depends upon your assignment and whether you are a teacher presenter, a small group discussion leader, or a team leader." How the applicant evaluates the merits of these different teaching assignments is not known. The administrator, however, knows that determining the number of teachers needed under a traditional system is much easier than doing so under a team program. Once again, deviating from the norm requires more decisions on the part of the administrator. As the number of possibilities for decision making increases, the potential for a positive influence of the administrator increases.

In the selection of new faculty members, the administrator needs to answer many questions. He needs to say what tasks must be performed. He must know what kinds of teachers can best perform the special functions in the instructional process. The way the morale of teachers already on the faculty is affected when a school presents team teaching is important. The administrator must, not only for himself but also for teachers and board members, justify his decisions concerning personnel policy. Wise administrators involve experienced teachers in the selection of new staff members.

COMPLEXITIES OF SCHEDULING

Most administrators are familiar with the schedule board and the conflict sheet, two devices used in developing a traditional teaching schedule. Such devices are not capable of resolving the more complex scheduling decisions inherent in team teaching. Even the use of the IBM 7090 computer with its capacity for storing and utilizing information will not resolve the myriad problems of an intricate team program involving large groups, small groups, individual study, overlapping periods and constant regrouping according to different abilities.

An effort is being made to resolve the complex team schedule problem by Dr. Robert Bush and Dr. Dwight Allen of Stanford University.* The identification of the variables that must be programmed to facilitate a fully flexible team teaching project is in itself a task of major dimensions. In the meantime, the administrator continues to serve as a human computer with less than perfect results in either efficiency of operation or economy of time.

Administrators going into team teaching programs would be wise to secure the services of a consultant on scheduling procedures.

Factors Which Affect Administrative Control

A universal human tendency, shared by administrators, is the expenditure of time and energy to influence more people or control a greater portion of the environment in which he lives. This tendency results in the establishment of rules, regulations, administrative procedures, patterns of behavior, channels of communication and systems of reward and punishment. These are inevitably coordinated to provide him with a greater measure of control over the school system. Team teaching represents a unique challenge to this tendency.

THE DECISION MAKERS

A long held point of view that boards of education should set policy, administrators should administer and teachers should teach is rapidly disappearing, if indeed it ever existed in practice. An administrator who strongly believes in centralization of control will find it harder to accept team teaching than one who accepts the concept of decision making at the operational level. Team teaching cannot flourish in a climate where all problems must be referred to the administrator for a decision before action can be taken.

Successful team teaching has the potential of modifying the decision making procedures of a traditional school, especially with regard to the instructional program. Decisions are made daily by the teaching team with regard to student grouping, use of facilities and subject matter taught. Teacher assignment, normally the domain of the administrator, is modified constantly by the needs of the team. Uniform teacher load gives way to demands of the team for more and better teacher preparation, for better utilization of teacher time, for fewer extracurricular assignments and for less non-teaching clerical-type duty.

* This research is part of Stanford's five-year Secondary Education Project, which is supported by the Ford Foundation's Fund for the Advancement of Education.

COMMUNICATION OF IDEAS

Vital to the control function are the channels of communication within the school. It is an easily understood principle that information is vital to the success of any endeavor. This is especially true of team teaching. In a traditional system it is important for the teacher and administrator to discuss classroom needs. Now teachers need to communicate with other teachers on the team as well as with the administrator about equipment and supply needs and facility changes. In addition, more frequent communication is needed between the administrator and teachers than before. Communication channels no longer serve as a primary means of control. Information available to teachers is obviously less usable as a medium of control by the administrator. Now the administrator must use more reason and judgment in making decisions. Information alone is less effective.

FLEXIBILITY OF APPROACH

Team teaching is a flexible approach to classroom instruction. It may take many forms. One form is to organize team teaching within traditional subject matter fields. As such, it is less disruptive and easier to implement. Methods of teaching rather than subject matter content are involved. Concentrating several United States History classes in one period to be taught by a team of teachers is less disturbing to teachers and therefore more readily accepted. Similarly, grouping English classes, science classes or physical education classes in one period can also be easily accommodated.

A less common and more difficult arrangement is the merging of subject matter fields such as English and social studies or science and mathematics, with team members coming from the respective subject areas. Possibly because such an approach is more disruptive to traditional organizational patterns and tends to diminish the separate identities of subject matter fields, its adoption is limited or the results are less well publicized—possibly both.

SPECIALIZATION OF PERSONNEL

Under the traditional system, a teacher serves as a jack-of-all-trades within his classroom. He lectures, leads discussions, supervises individual work projects, prepares audiovisual aids, corrects papers and performs a multitude of other clerical and semi-administrative tasks. His position, basically, is that of a director of learning in which he controls, within limitations, the learning of a given number of students within a subject matter field for a specified period of time. Such is not the case in team teaching. Specialization is the password and interpersonal relationships among team members the key to providing good learning experiences for students.

Who will give direction to the students' learning? "I will," says the teacher presenter who lectures to the large group. "We will," say the group discussion leaders who direct the interpretation of the material presented. "We will," say the teachers who supervise and correct the students' follow-up projects and class assignments.

Needless to say, the teachers of any team must work together in a planned and cooperative way if they are to be efficient as a team. Thus, specialization of function, thought to be the answer to more efficient use of master teaching personnel, may, because of inadequate team communication, prove to be less effective in helping students learn.

While the organization of a team may take many forms, administrative provision for effectiveness of the team, as measured by common planning periods, adequate aids, theme readers, individual student data cards, instantaneous flexibility of facilities and variable time modules, is most difficult to achieve. In fact, these limitations, along with experienced teachers incapable of adjusting to new situations, constitute serious deterrents to a successful team teaching program.

AVAILABILITY OF RESOURCES

As Winston Churchill said in 1941, ". . . give us the tools and we will finish the job." So it is with team teaching. No longer is the chalkboard enough; not that it ever was enough for the good teacher. Today the teacher must compete for the interest of students with Joey Bishop's latest program, an astronaut's flight around the earth and Ed Sullivan. The teacher specialist needs many resources to present involved concepts and conflicting ideas. The practice of using audiovisual resources only when the teacher felt inadequate to explain an idea or was unprepared has given way to their use to meet the need for providing more information to more people in greater depth, in a shorter period of time than ever before. This, plus our knowledge that children learn better that which they can hear, see, feel and smell makes telling, alone, a wasteful use of learning time.

EVALUATION OF PERSONNEL

The process of evaluating teaching and teachers is at best subjective in nature. The evaluation of team members by administrators is even more primitive. Specialization, an integral aspect of team teaching, makes evaluation of teachers more difficult; therefore, an administrator must have a rationale in evaluating the specialized contributions of each teacher. He must know what contribution the lecturer and the discussion leader make to the over-all success of team teaching.

Student reaction to team teaching provides an evaluation which may be of even more importance. Students in a plane geometry team teaching program at Glenbrook North High School,* in comparing team teaching to a traditional class approach felt: (a) the team teacher's knowledge about the individual student was less than average, (b) students did not have as much opportunity for individual help, (c) students had little desire to put forth effort and (d) the opportunity to receive help on homework was greatly reduced. In contrast, students felt that use of the overhead projector was very satisfactory, discipline was not a problem and the teacher's judgment on amount of homework to be assigned was above average. There were no significant reactions from parents regarding the team teaching program in plane geometry. No satisfactory administrative procedure for evaluating personnel in team teaching situations was developed. Evaluation of team members took place in traditional classes.

Provision for In-Service Education

The role of in-service education is becoming a more important part of the administrator's sphere of control and concern. While colleges have long provided pre-service education and in-service education associated with certification, less has been done to assist the teacher in meeting the challenge to ". . . do a better job with more students quicker." Notable exceptions to this include the workshops sponsored by the National Science Foundation. The John Hay Fellowships, the Advanced Placement Conferences and workshops sponsored by commercial firms such as the Shell Oil Company and General Electric Company are other exceptions.

In effect then, the local administrator is faced with retooling even as production, i.e., the education of children, continues. Budgetary provision by school districts for support of in-service education is by and large inadequate or non-existent. Some districts have provided funds to bring in, periodically, consultants to work with the ad-

---

* Partial results of a *Students Evaluation of Team Teaching* questionnaire administered in team teaching classes in plane geometry.

ministration and faculty in their retooling efforts. Often these efforts are sporadic, lack continuity and serve more as a public relations tool than as a real effort to initiate an in-service education program.

The administrator serious about initiating team teaching must be ready to devote considerable time to in-service education. Recruitment, easier than in-service education, is not the final answer. Chapter 6 discusses in-service program procedures in detail.

Balance—The Result of Successful Administration

The goal of administration, whether consciously stated or not, is most often related to maintaining a state of balance—a balance of the many operating forces, if you will. Whether this is desirable or not obviously depends on the definition of balance.

As used here, balance is defined as a state of moving equilibrium in which no function of the school, such as the athletic program, the academic curriculum, extracurricular activities or teacher comfort, is allowed to become so important that the direction and purpose of the school is significantly changed.

In appraising his school's current state of balance, the administrator will view team teaching in terms of its effect upon this balance and whether the effect is in the "right" direction.

QUALITY INSTRUCTION

All efforts to improve instruction must run the gamut of critical analysis. So it is with team teaching. A venture into team teaching poses some immediate, and for the most part, unanswerable questions. These are related to improvement of the quality of instruction and to whether students are learning more. Many schools report positive success with team teaching; others fail with it but don't have the desire to spread their failures across professional journals.

In one school a three-teacher team in algebra was disbanded after an extended period of time because of teacher disagreement over subject matter content and methods of presenting it to the students. In the English department, a two-teacher team was dominated by the male member of the team. Strengths of the other teacher were used sparingly or not at all. A four-teacher team in United States history became a three-teacher team halfway through the year when one member could not adjust to the decisions being made by the team. A three-person team in the fine arts area involving music, drama and art found initial, basic agreements difficult to achieve.

The above examples do not prove the unworkability of team teaching, for a certain lack of educational leadership was also noted on all these teams. The examples do show, however, that successful team teaching requires all of the ingredients of successful, traditional teaching, only more so.

To maintain instructional balance the administrator must be, and is, concerned with maintaining a high-quality instructional program. Team teaching must enhance the educational program, not detract from it. In many cases it has succeeded. In the others—well, maybe the administrator was inexperienced, had too few resources or too many limitations and not enough control.

SUCCESSFUL HUMAN RELATIONSHIPS

The complete transformation from a traditional approach to a team teaching approach is at best an evolutionary process when such factors as personnel, resources and facilities remain constant. When the administrator is able to change any of these factors, he is in a more favorable position to affect the balance of the educational program. The ability of the administrator to introduce team teaching without materially affecting the interrelationship of faculty members, may to a large degree determine the success or failure of the team teaching project. Without teacher support and cooperation, team teaching cannot possibly succeed.

Maintaining a state of balance within the school is also related to control of students. A common complaint heard among teachers is, "... the students have more freedom than we do." As one board member crudely and unthinkingly put it, "Whoever heard of the inmates running the place?"

If team teaching provides more freedom for the individual student, then the administrator can safely predict that a series of incidents, problems or disciplinary cases will arise. Unless care is taken to protect the teacher's traditional relationship with students by building student control measures into team teaching, a major pitfall may develop. Maintaining control of students poses a problem primarily in small discussion groups and during individual study where the student is motivated by a desire to express himself.

SUFFICIENT FINANCIAL SUPPORT

"He who pays the piper, calls the tune," goes an old saying. Indeed, it is a piece of wisdom that should be taken to heart by administrators, unless, of course, the school's major source of revenue comes from sources other than local patrons. Since this is not the case for most school districts, administrators are concerned about keeping voters, and parent voters in particular, happy and in a supportive frame of mind. Most of the school's public relations efforts, therefore, are oriented toward projecting a favorable image of the school in order to maintain voter confidence and to secure their "yes" vote.

Successful team teaching serves as a publicity vehicle for keeping the community attuned to school activities. It serves to publicize school efforts to keep pace with modern trends. It capitalizes on nation-wide publicity given to the endeavors of well-known schools in this regard.

A school can reduce the cost of education by providing one teacher, in a lecture situation, for classes of 50 to 150 students. This is not team teaching, however. Scheduling of three or four classes of thirty students together for a lecture followed by three or four discussion groups of thirty students is at best a modest approach and probably saves no money. Providing for discussion groups of fifteen students and supervision of individual student projects more nearly approaches one concept of team teaching, but may become more expensive in time and money. Therefore, the limitation of inadequate financial support, more than any other factor, prevents a school from initiating a team teaching project worthy of the name.

Another Look at Team Teaching

Team teaching, once an innovation, now a widespread practice, has yet to receive the distinction of being a permanent fixture on the educational scene. As a concept involving some general principles of learning, its potential remains unfulfilled. As an innovation depending primarily on local implementation and financial support, it is seriously hampered. By contrast, the new programs being developed in mathematics, science and foreign language under the auspices of the National Science Foundation are rapidly making an impact on the educational scene. The difference is related to the financial support given the content area innovations. The development of materials and the education of personnel are supported directly by the National Science Foundation. The cost of equipment purchased by the local school district is reduced by providing National Defense Education Act matching funds. Because of limits on local expenditures for equip-

ment, facilities, supplies and materials and for the in-service educa-
ton of teachers, team teaching may have less chance to survive than
other new programs.

Well-established programs of team teaching will continue in some
form or other. The extension of team teaching as a concept widely
practiced in its broadest meaning is not foreseen, however. Such an
extension might be possible if: (a) monies are made available to provide for the "pump-priming" stage, (b) enough data are collected
through research to establish team teaching as a superior method of
teaching, (c) team teaching programs provide for more individualized instruction, (d) colleges and universities develop programs
which prepare team teachers and (e) team teaching can be adapted
to the present structure of the school so as not to upset the state of
balance that exists.

Methods developed and controlled by subject matter specialists
under the auspices of agencies capable of providing long-term financial support may prove to be more enduring. Additional recent moves
in this direction include Project English and Project Social Studies
sponsored by the United States Office of Education.

Team teaching has made an impact, but, rather than altering the
instructional program nationally, it is being altered to fit local situations. While this facilitates the maintenance of local balance, the development of even newer approaches appears to be in the other direction. Much of the promise of team teaching rests with practicing educators in the schools across the land. It will be interesting to see if they
grasp the vision to make team teaching a permanent part of the
public schools.

CHAPTER 10

Qualities for Team Members

by

MELVIN P. HELLER

Dr. Heller has been associated with team teaching in a variety of capacities since its introduction in the schools. He served on the firing line as an assistant superintendent of schools when team teaching was inaugurated totally in his school. In another professional position Dr. Heller was a member of a research group which gave consultant services to school districts as they implemented team teaching and other instructional improvement practices. Currently he is serving as a professor of education at Loyola University, Chicago. In this role he is able to give consideration to the preparation of teachers for team teaching.

Melvin P. Heller received his doctorate at the institution he now serves as a faculty member. He has contributed a number of articles to professional journals on team teaching and is often quoted when the topic is discussed. He speaks authoritatively on staff leadership processes and teaching evaluation.

It is appropriate in any consideration of the effects of team teaching on teachers and, conversely, the influences of teachers on the concept that the subject should be discussed by Melvin Heller.

IF TEAM TEACHING is to be successful and lasting in a school, it needs more than enthusiastic reception by administrators and wholehearted sanction by a board of education. Successful teaming demands acceptance and even enthusiasm from teachers. Every team teaching enterprise is built on the character and competencies of the particular professional teaching staff using the concept.

The desire to improve professional competence by working co-operatively with others is the basic criterion for a teacher who is to be a part of team teaching. Ideally, team teachers would be the epitome of intellectual, professional and personal virtue. Actually, the qualifications of effective team teachers are not so demanding. In fact, the same qualities which make a teacher effective in a conventional setting make him effective in a team teaching situation. If unique qualifications were necessary for success in team teaching, the implementation of the concept would be futile for all but a select few.

In selecting teachers or in considering the possibility of becoming personally involved in teaming, it is sound to consider the emphasis of various personal and professional qualities for success in team teaching.

Intelligence, enthusiasm, curiosity, patience, understanding and imagination are, of course, important qualities of all teachers. Therefore, it is not necessary to elaborate on the obvious aspects of these qualities. It is significant, however, to note that few opportunities exist in a conventional school but abound in a team teaching situation to develop these qualities into special personal skills. Team efforts are strengthened as the members improve their professional and personal abilities. With practice and experience, one teacher may emerge as the expert at large group instruction. This teacher may develop excellent speech patterns, interesting humor, dynamic expository ability and a good theatrical sense. His performance before a large group might progress to be so outstanding that no other member of the team could equal his performance. Another teacher may become an expert without equal in guiding pupil-centered discussions, superior in the use of effective group dynamics and a subtle thinking guide rather than a mechanical force in developing viewpoints. Still another teacher may be most skillful in the guidance of pupil-centered, individualized activities. He will inspire a student to initiate projects, to do research and to write creatively.

While it is true that team teaching is a vehicle to conserve teachers' time through eliminating unnecessary duplication of effort, its dynamic strength develops from its ability to free each teacher to do the things he is best at doing in the instructional process. Anyone who gives serious consideration to team teaching needs to consider who can team teach. Is team teaching an appropriate organization for instruction for all teachers or for some teachers?

Experienced practitioners would agree that team teaching is not for all teachers. Some teachers do not seem to be able to share responsibility or to work harmoniously with other teachers in developing course goals and in carrying out instructional strategy. Only time and research will give us the final answers as to why everyone doesn't work successfully in a team. At this point we need to be satisfied with the empirical evidence that all teachers are not ideal candidates for team teaching.

No deprecation is intended when the contention is made that team teaching is not appropriate for all teachers. For example, the shy, the retiring, the introverted, the "lone wolf" teacher, however competent, probably would not be attracted to team teaching. Some teachers with years of effective teaching (as judged by competent observers) simply do not want to change their approach. Psychologically, a group of students is theirs, and to imply that a peer could share their zeal, effect and understanding is unthinkable for them. Since a major strength in team teaching is its emphasis on the individualizing of teaching and learning, it would be folly to insist that all teachers can be and should be team teachers.

Some conjectures, however, are in order. Those teachers who do not work well in teams are not to be identified by their number of years of teaching experience. The experience of Lakeview High School, Decatur, Illinois, showed that seasoned teachers with over twenty-five years of classroom experience did a superior job as team members. The supposition that it takes years of experience to be able to team is discredited by the experience at Ridgewood High School, Norridge, Illinois, where the staff was predominately an inexperienced one.

An analysis of the education of those successful in team teaching roles shows a diversity also. Some teachers do well on a team with only a bachelor's degree; others function profitably with a doctorate. Among successful and unsuccessful team members are both men and women. Moreover, those teachers with a predominate interest in students do as well as team members as those essentially interested in content. Inexperienced teachers often function successfully on teams with experienced teachers.

Teachers who are contributing team members and helpful to students are those who demonstrate a basic personal security. They are most often intellectually honest and confident of their knowledge and abilities.

Although team teaching does not call for more of the desirable characteristics of teachers than do other professional situations, it does highlight the absence of any of them. Among the necessary qualities of all good teachers several are worthy of note and elaboration.

Pliability and Creativity

It is important that the strong teachers maintain their strengths while they remain pliable enough to use their abilities in a variety of ways. The pliability necessary to maintain one's individuality while cooperating with others is a trait which can be developed. A team teaching situation offers opportunities to exercise and refine this ability. The planning phase alone requires team teachers to engage in a series of give-and-take thoughts and discussions.

Pliability deserves careful consideration. A pliable teacher will not allow his ego to suffer when his suggestions are not immediately acceptable to all members of the group. He will not be squelched easily and yet he will not thrust his point of view on his peers. Certainly, he will argue for what he believes to be correct, but there are many viewpoints which can be reconciled by a compromise. A pliable teacher will accept these compromises. His opportunities for creativity and individuality will become apparent during the aspects of the learning situation which he leads and directs.

Pliability does not mean spineless fluctuation. Pliability, as used in this context, is based on a respect for the worth of all members of the teaching team. The single best way to teach any subject is not yet known. In a team teaching situation the competent leader will have as many opportunities to use his talents as his ability and imagination will allow. Team membership will not stifle his creativity. In fact, a truly creative teacher cannot be stifled. Not only will his creativity shield him from academic suffocation, but it will become stronger in response to wholesome competition.

Although the creative teacher has much to offer his fellow teachers and his students, he cannot be given unbridled deferential treatment if any team effort is to be successful. An administrator may say, "I never give directions to creative teachers. I stay out of their way because I don't want to thwart their individuality." This view is an invitation to serious problems. Cooperative consideration and action are necessary if teaming is to be a profitable reality.

There is a great difference between a creative professional and a puerile pseudo-professional. Creativity is not license. It is not freedom to ignore obvious professional obligations. The school atmosphere must encourage creativity among the staff members. There is no dichotomy between authority and freedom to be creative. The *abuse* of authority leads to serious problems in a school as well as in our whole society, but the *need* for authority is obvious. The titles of superintendent and principal include some authority in their definition, semantically and legally.

In this light, the school environment should be permissive to the extent that no one is afraid to try out new ideas. If teachers have a right to be free thinkers, they have the obligation to respect that right in others. In order to guarantee these rights and their correlative duties in a team teaching situation, some structure is necessary so that order and direction are possible. This structure must be provided by the administration (with teacher suggestions incorporated), and it must be respected by the professional staff.

Rules and regulations which provide for close cooperation among team members should flow from this structure. These should provide guidelines for effective team involvement in the planning, the presenting and the evaluating of learning experiences. Adherence does not present a barrier to the creative activities of individual team members. In fact, the regulations which encourage close cooperation among team members can make the creative teacher secure in his creativity. In every phase of team teaching the talents of the creative teacher can be an asset to the team effort in vitalizing large group, small group and individual study instruction.

Leadership

As indicated, the creative teacher can add interest and depth to old ideas in novel ways. Although it would be ideal if all teachers were creative, it is no secret that many teachers are not creative at all. The leadership which creative teachers are able to provide can be a source of inspiration and professional improvement for the non-creative teachers.

Not all teachers wish to be leaders. A distinct advantage of team teaching is that it provides many opportunities for the development of teacher leaders. The teacher who is most proficient in a given aspect of a subject will become the leader during the time when that aspect is highlighted. If the team is organized to emphasize complementary strengths, all of the teachers will have an opportunity to lead some of the time. Doubtless, the run-of-the-mill teacher may lead less often than his more able colleagues, but this is as it should be. Mediocre leadership leads to mediocrity. Able leadership leads to improvement. Certainly, the run-of-the-mill teacher can benefit greatly from the leadership demonstrated by his more able, more creative team members.

The *average* teacher can improve his competence and classroom management skills through an association with team members. The average teacher may find that in some aspects of the curriculum he is the expert. He may find that no other teacher on the team had thought of enriching the history lectures through a study of musical themes popular during a given historical period. He may learn that his rock collection and his knowledge of geology make him a leader on the team in relation to that subject.

Merit recognition of peers is an invaluable aid to increased efficiency. Many average teachers are average only because they have not been inspired to overcome mediocrity. When given the chance to engage in intellectual discourse with fellow teachers, it may become apparent that each staff member has much to offer and that latent talents can flourish. In those areas where competence is lacking, the teacher can become the learner and gain from the knowledge of his colleagues.

In addition to these advantages, the *inexperienced* teacher can gain professionally from close contact with experienced teachers. Fortunately, the reverse is true, also. For example, a young, inexperienced teacher may have keen enthusiasm for and many new ideas about instruction but little knowledge of classroom management techniques. An older, experienced teacher may possess much knowledge of classroom management techniques, but his enthusiasm and originality may have faded. The enthusiasm of young teachers may be a tonic to the lethargy of seasoned performers.

Once the older teacher is aroused from his lethargy, the inexperienced teacher can learn about methodology, original approaches, organization, avoidance of pitfalls and disciplinary safeguards from the older teacher. Resulting contributions of each should be valuable to each other and most of all, to students. If these teachers have complementary academic strengths, the differences in their personalities may help each to become more effective with students.

The *poor* teacher creates the real problem in all teaching situations. The poor teacher who cannot be improved does not belong in any classroom. The poor teacher who can be improved has many opportunities for improvement in a team teaching situation. If a less able teacher is willing to learn, he can profit from intimate contact with fellow teachers. In a team situation shortcomings will become very apparent. In self-defense a poorly prepared teacher will add strength to his academic repertoire. At the very least he can imitate the good example of the creative, capable team members.

The in-service growth advantages of a team teaching situation can be a boon to the poor teacher. His gain in professional competence will benefit his fellow teachers as well as his students. No school can afford poor teachers. Team teaching will not solve all of the problems of the poor teacher, but it can provide ample opportunities to broaden teachers' knowledge and improve teaching skills.

Cooperation

Each team member must pay attention to the details which make a cooperative effort possible. Since several teachers are involved in each learning situation, *details which are minor in many schools become major in a team teaching situation.* Follow-up activities of all kinds can plague the teaching team unless great care is taken to insure that all involved are well informed. This cooperative effort does not force teachers into a single mold. It is not an attempt to shackle the mind of a teacher. Cooperation implies an opportunity to teach and to learn, to give and to get, and to increase the professional competence of all concerned.

Individuality will not be stifled if teachers develop a respect for the ability of the members of the teaching team, as well as the ability of their students. Free expression, broad and deep knowledge and a respect for others nourish teacher initiative and individuality. In case of disagreement among team members, the team leader or the principal should make the necessary decisions to get the team together. The importance of the decision making role will not only coordinate the plans of the teachers but will also involve the school leaders in the learning situation. Thus, the team approach adds a new dimension to the quality of cooperation.

Professionalism leads to a respect for the dignity and the importance of teaching. It encourages a conscientious effort at improvement and instills a sense of pride. It prohibits unprofessional conduct. Perhaps the quality is best described through a discussion of communications and inter-personnel relationships.

Effective communications are crucial in a team teaching situation. In any school situation communications are important, but in a team teaching situation the importance is highlighted. The success of a team is impaired when communications are not clear, free and open. Opportunities must exist for frequent formal and informal communications. Failure to notify team members of a change in plans, procedures or activities can have a deleterious effect on the team effort. This will negatively influence the instructional program. Confusion is obvious when a teacher who forgot to attend a planning session is not told that he is expected to lecture one week hence. If the team teachers work at it, there will be no problem concerning communications.

Team teachers must get along with each other. Gossip, petty differences, minor irritations and old wives' tales cannot clutter the communication channels. As the team teachers work ever more closely, they will learn many tidbits of information about each other. Prudence and discretion must guide them in their use of this information. Too often, the personal element beclouds the professional wisdom of a teacher. A team situation cannot endure if petty discussions reign. The more compatible the teachers, the less likely it is that they will have serious personnel problems.

Willingness to Change

The successful team teacher must view change in a favorable light. The chronological age of the teacher is not as important as his curiosity age. Any teacher, young or old, experienced or inexperienced, whose outlook permits change, experimentation and variation has the potential to become an effective team teacher.

Involvement in team teaching requires a new outlook on content, on methodology, on the roles of administrators, teachers, parents, and students. This new outlook will require the successful team teacher to accept the following:

1. Sometimes he will be a leader and sometimes he will be a follower in the school situation.
2. He can learn a great deal from others: fellow teachers, administrators and students.
3. Students can teach themselves many things which the teacher does not tell them.
4. Students require opportunities for self-development commensurate with their ability to assume these responsibilities.
5. It is necessary to plan, to prepare and to evaluate subject matter offerings in terms of large group, small group and individual study considerations.

These considerations represent change because they are not usual in the conventional school setting. For many people, change is anathema. A team teacher should not fall into this category.

If team teaching has any merit, the teachers involved must have more than a superficial interest in change. Their interest must be deeper than mere psychological involvement in change for its own sake. Their interest should be directed toward breaking the lock-steps of tradition in education for the purpose of improvement of the teaching-learning situation. A staff which is involved in team teaching can study issues and developments by relating new approaches, new methods and new structures to curriculum development and presentation. Once accepted, the changes required by team teaching can lead to an increase in intellectual curiosity, the development of new skills and the acquisition of knowledge on the part of administrators, teachers and students.

Importance of Orientation Programs

The foregoing comments highlight the learn-by-doing technique of developing those qualities which make team teachers successful. In addition to this type of in-service technique, orientation programs provide special opportunities to develop competence among the team members.

A well-structured orientation program can teach teachers by example how to lecture, how to conduct seminars and how to provide for individual differences. Not only can theoretical considerations be emphasized, but also practical experiences can be presented so that crucial insights can be developed. Among the kinds of considerations essential to a professionally profitable orientation program are these:

1. overview of the philosophy and the objectives of team teaching
2. the role of a teacher on a team
3. opportunities for teacher and pupil creativity, leadership and "follower-ship"
4. nature and techniques of large group, small group and individual study
5. differentiation possibilities in lectures, small groups and individual study
6. the use of audiovisual aids in large group, small group and individual study activities
7. group dynamics techniques
8. necessity for clear communications

The teacher new to the situation can learn excellent lecture techniques which he can emulate. He can also learn about mistakes which he is to avoid. As the orientation takes on the overtones of a workshop, teachers can have an opportunity to present some lectures as "trial balloons."

During the orientation period it is beneficial for all concerned to set aside time for small group discussions. During these discussions the teachers can learn much about technique and content relevant to team teaching. By doing, the teachers can learn much about group dynamics in an informal way. They can also learn that the group leader must guide the group toward its goal. Moreover, they can learn that there are many resources within the group and so a discussion group must not be monopolized by one, however competent he may be. Probably all concerned will realize that it is easy, although not desirable, for the leader of a small group to talk too much. If during the orientation period the leadership rotates, this lesson can be learned well. Through their participation, it will become clear to the teachers that seminars provide the opportunity to challenge, to question and to evaluate the concepts presented in lectures and derived from individual study pursuits.

In all probability, the majority of teachers new to seminar teaching will learn little more than obvious techniques, considerations and implications attendant to small group discussions. Nevertheless, this degree of learning can be very significant. However much the teachers learn during the orientation period will be an asset to the development of their managerial skills during the school year. By the end of the first school year some teachers will have developed to a high level of competence those skills, which they acquired initially during the orientation program. Thus, the value of such programs can be underscored.

CHAPTER 11

Team Teaching in the Content Fields

by

LORENE K. WILLS

Four years of visiting all types of schools and all grades from kindergarten through the sophomore year of college have taught Lorene K. Wills about all there is to know about what goes on in school. As general supervisor for the Office of Public Instruction in Illinois, she has come to be recognized as an authority on curricula. She speaks often before professional groups and writes for professional journals.

Mrs. Wills's graduate work was carried on at Teachers College, Columbia University, and Southern Illinois University, and she has been a teacher herself. In fact, her first experience with team teaching came when she participated in a common learnings program.

Currently Mrs. Wills is assistant county superintendent of schools in Golconda, Illinois.

Here she presents some results of her extensive observations and critical study of team teaching.

HISTORIANS WILL no doubt record the space flights of today's astronauts as one of the greatest achievements of the twentieth century. No one is apt to forget the thrill of hearing John Glenn's and Gordon Cooper's voices as they counted in unison to give Astronaut Cooper the signal to fire his retrorockets when the automatic controls on the Faith 7 went out. In every way, the perfect twenty-two-orbit flight of Cooper was a team effort. The Astronauts, crew, industry and even the tax-paying public make up a smoothly operating team whose achievements, as long as they work together, are limitless. "The sky is the limit" no longer applies to mankind's potential. Teamwork did it.

Similarly, public education is a team effort, yet the advantages of a united team approach have never been fully explored. This is especially true in two vital areas: the utilization of staff abilities and the use of community resources. By a careful analysis of the job to be done and by assigning the best-qualified individual or team to do it, the schools could operate much more productively.

Experience in many schools shows that teachers working together on projects which are constantly evaluated tend to grow professionally and to take an increased interest and pride in the quality of their contribution.

Surprisingly enough, when team teaching is used even the public seems to be better informed about the goals of the school. This public awareness may be due to the publicity surrounding the introduction of a new organizational pattern, or, hopefully, students may tend to become more interested and mature in discussing what they are learning with their parents who are naturally curious about the subject matter and the modern use of staff.

Acquiring and Retaining Content. Research through the years indicates that students highly motivated toward certain goals acquire more knowledge. Students also retain more if they use a variety of actions: discussing, hearing, seeing, feeling, writing, illustrating and doing.

In most of today's schools the student has ample opportunity to hear the teacher and to read a limited amount of material, mostly confined to one or more textbooks. All too frequently the library's accessibility is reduced due to the student's rigid schedule so that well-stocked shelves are virtually useless for his purposes.

Through flexible scheduling and a team approach more use can be made of library facilities. This can result in a greater depth of learning for the student as well as provide resources to take care of individual differences.

Curricular content should be divided into two fundamental parts: *basic content* for all persons and *depth content* for those with ability and interests that go beyond basic provisions.

Basic education should cover all subject areas—the humanities, social studies, languages, mathematics, science, fine arts and practical arts. The information should be up-to-date and required of all students. In each of these subjects, students with more ability should have opportunities to delve deeply—limited only by their own interests and abilities.

The content should give everyone a good basic background for decision making and should provide the students with more talent opportunities for further exploration. To accomplish these functions, schools must organize teachers into more efficient units, accept flexible scheduling, allow for large and small group instruction, free teachers from routine clerical duties, trust their professional judgment and reward them accordingly.

One pitfall to avoid in developing teams is to accept without question the premise that a highly motivated teacher will always be able to inspire students to achieve at a higher level. The student must be involved in the planning. Witness the teachers who travel during the summer and are shocked to find their classes are lukewarm to an intensive study of the beauties of the West or of Alaska. The great disappointment of educational television instruction arises from a lack of student involvement.

Content and Teaming

Goal-oriented instruction based on the student's needs and interests, with a high degree of involvement and with opportunities for independent research, is needed in a team approach to presenting content. Materials which invite reflection, interpretation or relating facts to each other should be provided.

What should the content include? John Dewey throughout his career insisted on "materials which at the outset fall within the scope of ordinary life-experience." He consistently urged "progressive organization of subject-matter."

During the block of time devoted to the disciplines, different kinds of experiences are to be provided—for learning the key concepts of the disciplines, for taking on the most significant facts making up a body of knowledge and for seeing the relationship among the various disciplines and their contribution to the totality of knowledge.

Planning the curriculum is a different task in a school utilizing the team teaching approach as it is in all schools. Since daily planning and readjustment among the team members are a continuous part of the team teaching process, this testing of ideas among fellow teachers and the continuous search for new techniques and materials integrates research, preparation and in-service study as part and parcel of the daily teaching job. Teachers are no longer required to plan on their own and then attend a department meeting where group planning takes place as something separate and apart from the teacher's own needs. Instead, teachers pool their resources to provide continuous, creative change and evaluation of curriculum for the benefit of students. The key factor is to think of the staff organization as clusters of professional persons assigned a collective responsibility to accomplish a given facet of the educational job.

Team teaching does break down the accustomed format for instruction. Flexible uses of time, space and personnel are permitted. The teacher-pupil relationship is changed. The format for curriculum development is modified. The organization should foster effective use of abilities and energy, in-service growth, teacher creativity, curriculum development and a good start for the beginning teacher.

Allowing time for active teacher participation and planning is not enough for success unless the teachers can work together effectively. Thus, teachers can learn only if given the opportunity to interact within the group. They must believe and experience the promise that a group product is usually better than the product of a single individual.

Team Teaching in the Elementary School. A teaching program whereby two, four or more elementary teachers exchange classes for special subjects can be a help to the teachers and can provide a more thorough education for the pupils. It is possible to find examples of efficient and effective cooperative teaching in every grade from kindergarten through college.

Team teaching can offer a method of total class organization. Teachers of adjoining rooms plan and work together so that pupils have a homeroom teacher and a reading teacher. The Joplin Plan by which pupils in grades four, five and six are regrouped into three groups according to reading achievement is an example of this kind of total-class organization.

Investigators seem to agree that homogeneous groups in reading are slightly superior to intact, ungrouped grades. Grouping for reading reduces pupil tension and is conducive to greater differentiation of instruction. With this plan, however, correlation with other subjects is difficult and cooperation among teachers must be superior.

The teacher, more than any other factor, determines the quality of elementary education. There is no substitute for a person sensitive to children and professionally trained to perform the teaching function. The teacher must value all children, and the pupils must sense the teacher's regard for them. The teacher is mainly responsible for the child's progress in acquiring academic skills and knowledge and simultaneously for his progress in developing the desire to learn, his growth toward effective citizenship and his increasing sensitivity to other people.

The elementary school, defined as a school extending through sixth grade, has changed greatly since the turn of the century. The content of instruction has greatly expanded. The elementary teacher is now being asked to prepare herself to teach the newer concepts in mathematics and science and, sometimes, to teach a foreign language.

Few educators in the elementary field would go so far as to advocate complete departmentalization of all subjects in the elementary school in order to lighten the load of the teacher. A very simple plan for exchange of classes for special subjects is the type of cooperative teaching most widely used at the present time. This plan seems to offer some relief for the teacher and provides a more thorough education for the pupils in the special subjects.

Several thousand schools are getting children together for large group instruction during a television broadcast after which the homeroom teacher supplements the lesson in the self-contained classroom. There is no reason why the educational television instructor could not work out a fine enrichment program with the regular teachers. Instruction in this manner holds much promise for elementary foreign language.

Another strength of the cooperative teaching plan is the amount of specialized equipment that can be made available for the use of teachers and pupils. Most schools would find it financially impossible to supply every classroom with a piano, a high-fidelity record player, a library of records and music books, but they could equip a room.

Teaming Helps Find the Right Plan

There is no pat formula for the right kind of organization in the elementary school. Each community and each school system has its own needs and priorities. But if elementary education is to be effective, more research and experimentation must be carried out in our schools. No one teacher can keep abreast of all the specialties. It seems, then, logical to assume that much greater use could be made of teaching teams in grades one through six.

In large city systems, two teachers are sometimes assigned to many of the self-contained classrooms because of the number of slow or non-readers in the slum areas of the city. These teachers work and plan together so that children can have more individual attention. One teacher will have three or four around her in the back of the room working on word attack skills while the other teacher is presenting a social studies lesson to the rest of the class. Expensive? Yes, but in the long run this is probably one of the most satisfactory ways of handling the potential dropout which Dr. James Conant calls "social dynamite."

This plan has the advantage of keeping the child in a familiar environment because stability in the early school years is essential if the child is to develop a sense of the world as basically orderly and predictable. It is also important at this crucial age for the child to have enough help to sense that he is making progress. No skill in education is more fundamental than reading. It is wise, therefore, to give the child help in acquiring this skill early in his school life.

In September, 1958, team teaching was introduced in four elementary schools in Norwalk, Connecticut. In the fall of 1961, this was extended to five additional elementary schools and one junior-senior high school. The program in the Fox Run School is carried on in all grades beyond the kindergarten. Dr. Harry A. Becker states in an article in the June, 1962, *Instructor Magazine*,

> Although there is still much to learn about team teaching, we have had enough experience to feel confident that it has genuine promise. While the shortcomings of the self-contained classroom plan of organization have long been known, there seemed to be no alternative. Today team teaching, or some modification of it, offers the prospect of a better organization for instruction. The Norwalk Plan of team teaching may make it financially possible for school systems in the average range of financial support to institute a new organization.

These are some of the advantages for a team teaching approach in the upper grades of the elementary school:

1. Team teaching facilitates grouping. In the self-contained classroom it is often not practical to group for instruction other than reading.
2. Pupils spend more time having instruction than when they are in a self-contained classroom. The more grouping done in a self-contained classroom, the more time each pupil must spend doing routine "seatwork." In team teaching, while one teacher is busy

with one group, the other teachers can work with the rest of the students.

3. Teachers in a self-contained classroom have so many things to do that they lack the time to prepare lessons which use such modern teaching aids as overhead projectors and other audiovisual aids.

4. Team teachers are in a better position to make careful preparations for teaching. Those for which each has major responsibility are likely to be in subject areas in which he has the most strength and security. Each member of the team is responsible for planning fewer lessons.

5. The position of the team leaders offers opportunity for promotion which does not require the teacher to leave teaching for an administrative position. It carries increased status and prestige.

6. The teacher is relieved of routine chores and clerical work.

7. Teachers work together in such a way that they can influence each other. This is helpful for the new and experienced teacher.

8. The principal is relieved of routine duties by the team leader; therefore, he can concentrate on broad educational planning for improvement.

Team Teaching in the Junior High School. Junior high school personnel, realizing the success of the block of time or multiple period and noting a widespread interest in team teaching, have combined the two to offer a promising plan for improving classroom instruction by the more effective use of teaching personnel and of time. The team teaching program has two main objectives at the Junior High School level: (1) to make maximum use of teacher time by developing a flexible schedule for instruction which provides opportunities for teams of teachers to present large group lectures, small group seminars and tutorial services to students when needed and (2) to provide a program of student grouping which allows the subject matter to be geared as closely as possible to the abilities of the student.

Junior high schools have developed many different programs to meet the main objectives of flexibility of instruction and optimum use of teacher time. Griffin Junior High School, Los Angeles, California, has a program typical of many in the United States. The teachers involved in team teaching meet with their individual classes for two consecutive periods or block of time. Once or twice a week, or even more often, depending on the nature of the subject and the material to be covered, the teachers combine classes in one room. The groups when combined for large group instruction average around seventy in number. One teacher will present the material for the two groups, and the other will be circulating, encouraging, guiding, helping individuals or listening. Each teacher is constructively critical of the other when they meet later to evaluate and plan.

Team Teaching in the Senior High School. Continued examination of present instructional practices in the secondary school and experimentation with various approaches to the teaching process are essential if the schools are to keep pace with the explosion of knowledge and if maximum effectiveness of the learning outcomes is to be realized. Team teaching minimizes the possibility of mediocre instruction.

At Ridgewood High School, Norridge, Illinois, a team is not necessarily composed only of members of the same subject area, for example, a science team or a history team. At Ridgewood the teams are broader in scope and are classified as humanities and math-science teams. A humanities team consists of teachers of history, English, music, art and various foreign languages. A math-science team includes teachers of biology, mathematics, industrial arts, home economics, business education and physical education.

The personnel of this school feel that there are advantages to this type of organization. The team approach uses to best advantage not only the major teaching knowledge of each staff member, but also the special interest areas he may have pursued in conjunction with or in addition to his major teaching area.

At Ridgewood teachers are supported by an adequate staff of specialists—clerical, secretarial, student assistants and teaching interns. For example, a teacher desiring an overhead projector needs only to present a sketch and a description of what is desired to the audiovisual secretary. This secretary does all the artwork and actually produces the finished visual. Likewise, tests may be composed by a teaching team, but they will be typed and reproduced by a clerical assistant.

At Ridgewood each teacher is provided with a block of time to perform the professional duties in connection with team teaching. Some of the blocks are as long as three hours. It has been their experience that these blocks of time are far more productive than are the usual isolated forty- or sixty-minute "conference periods" usually provided in the conventional schedule.

A continuous analysis is being made of the activities of the different kinds of groups operating at Ridgewood—large groups, discussion groups, laboratory groups, study groups and project groups. On the basis of this analysis, the schedule provides for time allotments which are most appropriate to the group's activities.

Size of School and Teaching Teams. Sometimes the question is asked, "Can a small school organize its teachers into teaching teams?" Good illustrations can be given of teaching teams for schools of varying enrollments.

Naturally, a large school has an advantage when setting up teaching teams. There are more opportunities simply because the staff is larger and more varied.

A small school with an enrollment of 300 or less could start experimentation with team teaching in the required courses such as English, American History or physical education. If the faculty and students are happy with their experiences, the program can be expanded.

The Need for Careful Planning

Assuming that the school and community climate is favorable toward experimentation in team teaching, what specific steps must be taken to initiate a program? These may be some of the steps:

1. An experiment should grow out of the needs and interests of the staff and student body. The principal must stimulate and guide these interests and not wait for them to crop up.
2. Careful planning and preparation should precede the launching of any experiment. Such planning must include a clear definition of goals, a specific plan of organization and procedures for attaining goals, the types of pupils to be included in the projects, the controls to be set up and the methods of evaluation.
3. Perhaps the most important factor in determining the success of an experiment is the teaching staff selected for it. At no time should an experiment be forced upon teachers, nor should it threaten the security of other teachers who are doing a satisfactory job.
4. The principal must provide material incentives for experimentation. Experimentation demands extra time, effort and energy.
5. The principal should keep the faculty informed about the nature and progress of the experiment.

Experimentation should constitute a regular and significant aspect of a school's investment in education. Team teaching can be used in any subject and in any school. Let us not become so afraid of failure that we attempt nothing new.

CHAPTER 12

A Summary of Team Teaching— Its Patterns and Potentials

by

VIRGINIA M. CASEY

Lakeview High School at Decatur, Illinois, is one of the few schools in the country to organize its entire curriculum around the team teaching plan, with small group and large group instruction.

As head of Lakeview's English Department, Virginia M. Casey has been wholely involved in team teaching as both teacher and supervisor. She was a member of the pioneer group which began a team teaching project in 1959.

In addition, Miss Casey has a full understanding of the secondary school English curriculum and has helped prepare curriculum guides for the Illinois Department of Public Instruction.

In this chapter, then, Miss Casey presents, from her years of successful experience, an overview of team teaching principles.

BEST THING that ever happened!"

"Won't work; it's too much like college."

"Our whole faculty is invigorated by team teaching."

"Just wishful thinking—not practical."

"I wish they'd just let me teach."

"Good to begin with, it's getting better—and there's plenty of the 'best' to shoot for."

So runs the gamut of reaction, from praise to abhorrence, from hesitation to exultation, to this latest upstart in secondary school curriculum, team teaching. Designed to meet the current crisis of enlarged populations and resistant financial support, as well as to advance quality education, team teaching has become the center of controversy.

The description of a team teaching system presented in this chapter approximates what teachers experienced with the concept seem to approve. This, then, may serve as a model for consideration.

The classroom teacher with the "Knock before Entering" sign on the door may react with skepticism; the curious teacher may approach the topic with hesitation, with truculent demands for more information. The teacher using this new method successfully is often so elated and challenged by his experiences that he tends to rationalize all objections with such comments as, "People are usually down on things they aren't up on."

Now, the success of the team teaching movement is not going to rest on skillful eavesdropping or elaborate opinionnaires, but the intensity of feeling and the volume of the questions being asked show the great interest in the method and expose the underlying drive of professional teachers to seek ever new and better ways of instruction.

Of course, the idea of teachers working as members of a team is not a new idea. Extracurricular programs often depend on shared responsibilities. Special committees thrive on combined talents. Within the classroom itself, team teaching in a mild form may be observed in the occasional sharing of unit activities between two compatible teachers or in the exchange of teaching duties for the mutual benefit of two groups of students.

Team teaching, however, implies an all-out effort on the part of two or more teachers who assume responsibility in a coordinated program of instruction for the same group of students. Team teaching combines the best talents of a group of teachers, freeing them for the exclusive discharging of professional duties in order to serve youth better. Thus, the optimum specialization of skills, added incentive in the interplay of minds and increased availability of teachers for individual help to students are achieved.

This new program of team teaching vitally changes the role of the teacher in the learning process. As a result, one can see emerging an organizational pattern, an operational pattern and an instructional pattern which are all unique.

Organizational Pattern of the Team

Generally speaking, teaching teams used most frequently consist of all the teachers of a given subject. They meet together under a chairman and cooperatively plan content and procedure, both long range and immediate. They are joined by aides, or paraprofessionals, who assist the process in a semi-professional or clerical way.

The professional members are titled teacher-presenter (TP) and teacher-instructor (TI). They are generally considered of equal rank and importance, although the teacher-presenter is more likely to be chairman of the team. Some schools may give status to the presenter through a higher salary, although the major difference between the teacher-presenter and the teacher-instructor is only the special area of instruction that each is responsible for. The TP influences the collective instructional progress of the course while the TI deals with students on a highly individual basis.

Specifically, the TP is the person whose central concern is giving students maximum instructional development. He assumes responsibility for the over-all planning of the course and, because of this, is likely to serve as chairman of the teaching team. He presents content material in lectures to large groups of students and re-enforces his lectures with suitable audiovisual aids. Testing and evaluation of pupil progress is in his province, particularly on material directly related to lectures. Often, however, final grades are given by those teachers who have small groups; they consider grades for small group participation and look at evidence of learning from independent study projects.

The professional requirements for teacher-presenter include a master's degree, wide knowledge of subject matter, previous teaching experience, leadership ability, organizational skill, communicative skill, stamina and a willingness to "go the extra mile."

Specifically, the TI is the person whose instructional focus is on providing for the individual differences of students. He must be adept at analyzing learning problems and motivating students to perform. Expert at discussion techniques, ideally, he helps students express themselves skillfully and investigate resources imaginatively. He contributes to the plan of the lecture and, if aides are not available, assists in preparation of materials to supplement the presentation. The TI's presence in the large group lectures is valuable for proper coordination of the team's effort in follow-up activities and for maintaining rapport between *all* team members and the students of that particular subject. Sometimes, he operates equipment or helps to dispense materials.

A master's degree may be a part of the TI's professional requirements, but not necessarily so. The ability to draw people out is basic. His interest in children should at least equal his interest in subject matter. Above all, a TI is judged on his willingness to cooperate.

The non-certified members of the teaching team are the instructional aide, the clerk and the general aide, who do service jobs. They carry out mechanical functions so that the teachers can devote full time to planning and instruction. They do not originate, create or develop policy; they carry out the agreed-upon program, assisting and strengthening the work of the professional teacher. Some knowledge of subject matter, especially from a technical point of view, is desirable. They are responsible to the teacher-presenter and handle such activities as theme correcting, drafting of bibliographies, producing illustrative materials, collecting and recording, typing, duplicating and filing. Taking roll, monitoring and equipment operation may be assigned to them also. Salaries are commensurate with their duties.

Job specifications for team members vary with the size and requirements of the school and sometimes with the abilities of the teachers. Larger schools may have six to eight members on the team, while smaller schools may only support two or three. Sometimes the roles of teacher-presenter and teacher-instructor are held rigidly; often they are exchanged to take advantage of one teacher's superior skill or more extensive knowledge in a specific subject area.

It seems to be important to students that each team teacher occasionally assume the role of "presenter" in a lecture. This experience is wise, also, from the standpoint of team planning and evaluation. Conversely, the teacher-presenter can guide progress much better if he conducts regularly at least one small discussion group. A last reason for some exchange of roles is the welcome change of face and pace for teachers and students.

The role of the administrator is both succinct and vital in a team teaching program. In addition to active leadership in the area of ideas, his greatest contribution is in providing a climate for healthy democratic growth, in which ideas can be expressed, plans integrated and evaluation geared to producing a workable design. Then team teaching becomes a meaningful challenge to everyone involved.

Operational Pattern for the Team

The specialization of teaching roles requires basic changes in class scheduling and in student grouping. Flexibility becomes an important consideration. The daily schedule gives way to a weekly pattern, with classes meeting in varied-sized groups throughout the week and repeating that pattern each week.

In a team teaching system the unit of time in a day is often between twenty and forty minutes—much less than in the traditional setup. This permits some classes to be one unit, or module, long; others can be a combination of two or three modules in length. Thus, not all students move when a bell rings, nor is every class of the same length.

New patterns of instruction are concerned with three basic activities tied to three different student environments: content presentation in lectures to large groups; discussion in small groups; and creative exploration in independent study. And for exceptional situations a fourth, medium-sized group can be organized.

The percentage of time for each activity in the total week's program will vary. However, a general breakdown might be 20 per cent spent in large group lectures (held two or three times a week), 50 per cent spent in small group class (held alternately with lectures and for longer periods of time) and 30 per cent in independent study (arranged according to the individual student's schedule).

Length of the Class

The length of the class is determined by the intended nature of the learning experience. Content presentations, often in capsule form, require intense concentration from students. These presentations can be relieved somewhat by vocal emphasis, examples, maps, graphs, graphic illustrations and other visual aids, as well as audio devices, such as records or tapes. But these are a calculated portion of the total message, not gimmicks. They give a quick change of pace but still continue to tax the average student's short attention span. For most fruitful results, therefore, brief lectures become the rule rather than the exception.

The situation is somewhat different for the small group class. Direct participation, involving as it does the ego, sharpens the student's motivation. Competition, as in drill, debate or reporting, heightens interest. The wide variety of activities possible and the more leisurely pace invite a renewal of attention should his attention lag.

There is a practical need, too, for more time in the small group class, time for analysis of points presented in lecture, for clarification, for application, for judgment. Here is the place in the schedule for drilling in mathematics, checking worksheets in vocabulary, learning from tapes in language laboratory, doing experiments in science, manipulating materials and tools in home economics or industrial arts, comparing maps in economic geography, applying ledger principles in bookkeeping, and so on. Thus, these classes meet for a longer time.

Independent study, whether a follow-up of class assignment or a creative exploration, is conducted on the student's own time. The length of time will vary with the ambition and schedule of the individual student.

THE GROUP SIZE

The group size is determined by the learning activity. Since the function of the lecture is to present basic content or, at times, enrichment, this can be done as easily with large numbers of students as with more limited numbers. Thus, 200 or more students in a lecture can be handled easily. Medium-sized classes of fifty to seventy-five students are sometimes formed for semi-presentation combined with more traditional teacher-student communication or sub-group discussion. Demonstrations in meal preparation, electronics or typing procedures are considered practical with this group size.

Discussion involving analysis and interpretation, or individual help in skill mastery, requires a very small group, preferably no more than fifteen students. This group is then often subdivided to make work even more feasible. Ability grouping in the small group pattern makes instruction easier but increases the complexity of the scheduling process.

Conclusion. The flexible pattern of scheduling, while a knotty administrative problem, has these distinct advantages for the teacher:

1. It permits the teacher to concentrate primarily on a particular teaching skill. Some master teachers are excellent at both lecturing and at leading discussions, and are equally adept at all phases of their subject. Most teachers, however, excel in one skill or one area. Team teaching permits the most efficient use of teacher talent through specialization of teaching roles and custom-sized groups.

2. It provides ways of meeting the individual needs of all student intellectual levels by allowing a schedule that works for the teacher, rather than confounding his problems.

3. It utilizes staff time to advantage by providing large blocks of time in a teacher's week for professional planning and preparation. It does this by handling large groups of students in one-shot presentations, replacing the wearisome repetition of traditional schedules.

4. It helps the teacher do a better job of instruction by isolating the strengths and weaknesses of both teachers and students. Thus, strengths are reinforced and weaknesses bolstered.

Instructional Pattern for the Team

Teaching is essentially creative. It becomes significantly more so with the added opportunities for new approaches and the shifting focus in course content. The entire cooperatively conceived plan becomes unit-based, with a certain portion assigned to large group presentation, another portion allotted to small group activities and the third part designed for independent study. Planning which brings about the proper division of the unit, followed by the coordination of the separate activities into an integral whole by the student as he assimilates the parts, is indeed a tremendous problem for the team. And this basic planning must go on before one lecture of the unit is given. What makes the content and what makes the footnote?

Evolving from the storm of creativity are the following variations in content and method.

CHANGING CONTENT OF LARGE GROUP LECTURE

Teacher-centered instruction is given formally to large groups of students who listen, take notes and study the material presented. Here the teacher-presenter, following the teaching team plan, will indicate course goals and suggest a sense of direction toward their attainment; present ideas given in reading material as overview, analysis, clarification, reinforcement, supplement or summation; develop background for understanding new concepts, authors, techniques; call attention to continuity within and relationship across subject matter lines; enrich basic content with depth of thought or strength of effect; associate new skills and ideas to past experience of students; illustrate ideas presented with a variety of audiovisual aids; utilize the best techniques in the practical skills of reading and speaking; share the excitement of learning in all phases of the subject; and evaluate student comprehension and mastery of concepts and skills.

Lectures should have a crisp, easy-to-remember continuity, but one which will allow embellishment. Each lecture must be a precise lesson in itself while being correlated within a broader unit taking in all the follow-up activities. The teacher-presenter should build in these mechanisms of learning: classification, association, assimilation and memorization. Transparency cards prepared ahead of the lecture can virtually set the sequence and dramatize the development.

CHART I

FORMAT OF LARGE GROUP LECTURE

I. INTRODUCTION
    A. Announcements of general items
    B. Advance assignment
       (good to give this early)
    C. Topic of lecture
       1. Goals of lecture
       2. Text reference
    D: Outline of points to be covered.

II. MAIN DEVELOPMENT
    A. Basic content in planned order
       (points from projected outline or from points given as lecture proceeds)
    B. Accompaniment
       1. Illustrations to capture interest, clarify, enrich, apply (pointer can be used to focus attention to item or area)
       2. Other audiovisual aids, whole or in part
       3. Shared activity, as dramatization

III. CONCLUSION
    A. Summary of points made during lecture
    B. Dispensing of worksheets, discussion guides, bibliography, suggestions for independent study

---

IMPLICATIONS OF LARGE GROUP STRUCTURE

Until a teacher is faced with a teacher-presenter role, he might not realize these implication of large group structure:

1. Large group presentation is a unique structure.
    Lecture is more closely related to a formal speech than to an informal explanation.
    Content must have "meat" in it—not just interesting asides.
    Material can be aligned with text matter but should not be a

slavish recital (student can read text without attending lecture).

Text should be used as one of many important resources or refences; the student's lecture notebook becomes the course guide.

2. Motivation must be built into the plan.

Value placed on large group lectures in the total course activities arouses attention.

Fast pace and relatively short span holds attention.

Pertinent examples, intriguing questions and flashes of humor add interest.

Areas for further thought, exploration and application must be incorporated for proper motivation.

In general, a business-like, concise, hard-hitting approach is necessary for facile note-taking.

Discipline problems during a good lecture are practically nil.

3. Lecturing places a premium on organization of ideas.

Planning is concerned with unit ideas, often thematic.

Details should develop essential phases of topic.

Follow-up activities must be integral part of unit.

Each lecture must be important in total content design.

4. Record should be kept of lecture presentations.

Composite activities should form part of team's resources.

Copy of lecture should be available to all team teachers before or immediately after presentation.

Tape recording of lecture may be used for critical evaluation as well as for student referral use.

5. Illustrations should accompany lecture presentations.

Retention is increased significantly with their use.

Artistic illustrations dramatize unit.

Thinking ability and note-taking skills are improved.

6. Good speech habits are required.

7. Special listening and note-taking skills must be taught to students.

8. Student's notebook should be checked from time to time to detect weaknesses and strengths in note-taking.

Purposes of the Small Group Class

The small group is student-centered. It is focused on teaching students to grasp the intelligent means by which knowledge is gained, in the hope that they will become active instead of passive learners. To that end, the teacher-instructor seeks to —

clarify points from content presentation in large group without repeating the lecture;

adjust activities to type of learning indicated by the nature of the material; e.g., skill-mastery or idea-comprehension;

gain insight into group motivation through careful study of behavior;

share interpretations, both professional and student, for deeper understanding and appreciation;

broaden and enrich ideas and concepts introduced into the course in large group lecture;

encourage active participation and leadership by all members;

promote mutual listening skills on part of both teacher and student;

support individual questioning;

develop critical reading, logical thinking and scientific inquiry;

strengthen basic skills in self-expression, in both speaking and writing;

help the group solve problems bridging their interests and the interests and demands of the times;

establish a tolerant atmosphere where beliefs, values and prejudices can be examined intelligently;

assist each person in developing new ways to evaluate himself;

motivate students to explore further in worthwhile and related independent study and help them gain the skills for doing so;

be available for individual student conferences.

The basic tenet of the small group pattern is that the student will learn by using ideas presented to him during the large group lecture. While oral discussion is the most dynamic technique, it is not the only learning activity.

ACTIVITIES OF SMALL GROUP

1. Activities for entire small group (usually in circle or seminar arrangement:
   verbalizing understandings and relationships; building concepts; questioning and challenging ideas;
   clearing up misunderstandings or gaps in information;
   applying basic information to specific problems;
   enriching experiences through guests, reports, programs, trips;
   evaluating group progress.
2. Activities for sub-groups (2-5 students suggested):
   discussing portions of over-all topic for later report to larger group;
   studying together; checking mastery of skills; drill exercises; reviewing;

working together on group project;

receiving special help from teacher on "blind spots."

3. Activities for individuals:

preparation and follow-through on assignments;

engaging in solo creative project;

studying for test; testing; self-analysis;

receiving individual help from teacher.

IMPLICATIONS OF THE SMALL GROUP PATTERN

The job of the teacher-instructor is so strategically placed that the implications of the small group pattern quickly become obvious to him:

1. TI must learn as much as he can about students from guidance folders, observation, conferences, tests.
2. TI is link between lecturer and student; he must be able to implement the plan well and promote human relationships by cooperating fully with team members.
3. TI must be master at group dynamics, knowing when to talk and when to keep still (latter is harder part).
4. TI must have rapport with students to be able to help them develop to full potential.
5. TI should evaluate wisely for he is in the best position for judgment.

Independent Study

This is the third prong of the new pattern of instruction. It seeks to enlarge the capacity for self-development through fruitful work undertaken by the student because he feels a need for it, and by creative endeavor because he has the interest and talent to pursue further goals.

Since, generally speaking, approximately one-third of a student's time is involved in independent study, responsibility is placed on the teacher—

to inculcate in students a desire to master material and skills;

to develop in students desire to go beyond basic content;

to allow leeway for creative exploration in planning of units; to offer suggestions for projects within units;

to serve as a resource person, directing students to purposeful reading and research;

to hold students accountable for work in this phase of the program.

Additional Changes for Team Teaching

Instructional success requires that all possible resources be brought into play. The program delineated by competent personnel and made operational by flexible scheduling and grouping still requires architectural changes to become practical. Adding partitions or removing walls for varied-sized classes, assigning areas for team meetings and enlarging library facilities are acceptable innovations; planning a new building with specific actions tailored to fit the team teaching program is most desirable.

Perhaps the most dramatic innovation in team teaching is the special equipment for large group lecturing. Here the center of attention is the transmission center equipped with mike, speaking stand, overhead projector and screen, recording equipment and suspended mirror for close viewing of demonstrations. Facilities for other kinds of audiovisual aids from the floor should also be available. Student chairs should facilitate note-taking. Adequate acoustics are important. Sliding doors for sub-dividing lecture room and converting the area into medium or small group rooms make for a versatile arrangement.

The instructional materials center is the "library of the future" and becomes the true core of the school. In addition to a full complement of regular library resources, the IMC has records, tapes, films and filmstrips catalogued and available for showing to individuals or groups. Conference rooms serve small groups and individual study carrels promote independent thinking.

One of the biggest boons to teachers is the teacher's workroom area. Here members of teams may meet and plan; here illustrative materials may be prepared and the work of paraprofessionals may be done. This follows the premise that good teachers must have facilities and materials to do a professional job.

A large number of audiovisual aids promises useful and dramatic results. These include an electronic learning laboratory for personalized two-way communication with use of tapes, open and closed circuit educational TV channels, programmed instruction machines and materials, use of dictaphone for improving quality of compositions and a developmental reading laboratory.

Recent refinement of processes and improvement of materials are making possible better transparencies for overhead projection in lectures. Producing negative and positive images, overlays of sequential effects, colored-ink illustrations and transfer of clay-based pictures directly from their source to a plastic sheet are fascinating and worthwhile. To these must be added the use of double-image projection for comparative or panoramic results.

Potentials of Team Teaching

It is much too early to give an authoritative evaluation of team teaching, for it is still too immersed in a period of adjustment, of growth, of anticipation. One can, however, make certain observations based on effects now beginning to show.

The first consideration is the common denominator of all educational effort: the development of the student. How, then, does the student benefit from team planning beyond the results expected in a good traditional set-up?

The student is able to get (from large group lectures) a more comprehensive view of a whole unit of work before tackling its separate parts; he is skillfully directed in mastering important details and in thinking critically; and he obtains a sense of closure as an evaluative summary is given.

There is good evidence that this program increases the student's involvement in his own learning by arousing his intellectual curiosity; by encouraging him to set his own goals, organize steps and assimilate points; by training him to reach for concepts beyond the facts, to seek a wide variety of resources and to correlate and see relationships across subject matter lines.

It trains him to listen effectively, to take part fruitfully in democratic discussion and to assume leadership roles. Although independent and creative thinking is emphasized, the student can have a private conference at any time with any number of the team. Thus, intellectual stimulation of students by contact with the several personalities of the teaching team is increased.

Intellectual freedom and quality learning are natural products of the team system because the team utilizes its best talent at the most opportune time.

The second consideration is the extent to which a teacher can perform more effectively. Designed to aid the teacher to do a more professional job, team teaching rearranges time, functions and values.

Adjustment to this new order is not easy. The beginning teacher is, at present, rarely prepared to perform in a team teaching system, while the experienced instructor may feel uncomfortable. Surrender of autonomy to the group effort is for some teachers intolerable, even traumatic.

Often with full awareness of the job dimensions and with the earnest desire to work cooperatively, teachers find many areas of difficulty. Insecurity with new methods, breaking away from text-books in favor of wide use of resources, the depersonalization of the classroom and the disclosing of "pet" ideas in team planning can only result in a sense of loss. Compound this with the insistent demands on energy, time and talent in preparing quality work—coupled with impatience due to relative slowness in group decision-making, with the "humiliation" of subduing the ego in favor of the group will, with the requirement to take criticism of colleagues as well as give it, with extra attention needed to learn student abilities and work habits—and the success of team teaching may be shadowed, perhaps endangered.

Happily, the credits promise to outweigh the debits. The master teacher can think like a manager, not like a technician of publisher-dominated texts. His sense of usefulness is increased as he makes full use of his abilities in producing creatively and in maintaining a meaningful place in the team organization.

He shares in the fellowship and contagion of enthusiasm which can weld together an entire faculty. His participation in decision mak-ing can do much to generate self-confidence. The new approaches awaken the imagination and stimulate discovery. Specialization of jobs permits focus or concentration on specific areas, while release from mechanical chores provides time and energy for superior teaching.

His motivation of students becomes more effective as the teacher learns more about their capabilities, the ways in which they learn and the materials to which he can refer them. And when student in-terest becomes self-generative, teaching becomes sheer joy.

The team teacher thus becomes more skilled and better informed as he stretches a little higher in performance and rethinks the con-cept of success.

Finally, the changing role of the team teacher is affected by a basic educational goal.

One of the teacher's greatest responsibilities is to help students pass from one indispensable stage of growth to another as realistically and as orderly as possible. A certain amount of frustration and turmoil is necessary and incident to the process of growth. When any part of that process is truncated, the student may be prevented from proper psychological transition.

Any teacher worth a new grade book each year will help the student find himself and develop responsibly. He can best do this by himself becoming a disciplined, self-governing personality.

Here members of the teaching team can help each other to achieve greater maturity by agreeing with each other to do so. And the dividends will be passed on to the students in a truly co-operative venture leading them to healthy "adult-centered" futures.

Now all of these admirable objectives are in the goal-lexicon of the traditional program, but somehow in the team teaching pattern they receive a primary emphasis and, in the enthusiasm of operation, appear to be more vigorously sustained. Certainly an important change with the power to reach individuals is influencing education today.

Team teachers know where they are leading, and they are working intensely to find the best way to get there. It is not a simple project, but it is a tremendously satisfying and challenging one. Why don't you try it and see for yourself?

TEAM TEACHING BIBLIOGRAPHY

Compiled by Anne Kavanaugh, University School, Indiana University

(These abbreviations are used in the following material: Elem. = Elementary; Sec. = Secondary; Jr.H.S. = Junior High School; H.S. = High School; Jr. Coll. = Junior College.)

Adams, Andrew S., "Operation Co-Teaching, Dateline: Oceano, California," *Elementary School Journal* 62:203-212, January, 1962. Article is concerned with a variety of topics, but especially good is its discussion, in length, of the tremendous advantages over a one-room regular class, using illustrations. (Elem.)

Aden, Robert C., "Team Teaching at North Texas University" (1960-61), *Peabody Journal of Education* 39:283-287, March, 1962. Team teaching experiment with Social Studies student teachers. (All levels.)

Allen, Dwight W., and Moore, Robert B., "Talents, Time, Tasks, and Teachers," *California Journal of Secondary Education,* 35:232-235, April, 1960. Introduction to symposium reports, concentrating in these few pages on team teaching concept and ways to develop it more fully. (Sec.)

Anderson, Robert H., "The Junior High School," *Architectural Record 129*:126-131, January, 1961. Description of "middle school unit," non-graded schools, teaching teams, "continuous education." (Jr.H.S.)

————, "Team Teaching," *Education Digest 26*:5-7, May, 1961. Results, advantages and problems. (All levels.)

————, "Team Teaching in Elementary School," *Education Digest 25*:26-28, November, 1959. Brief summary of some outcomes of mass project, giving special note to personnel grouping and advantages and changes needed yet. (Elem.)

————, "Team Teaching," *NEA Journal 50*:52-54, March, 1961. Discussion covering aspects of area of team effort. Describes Lecupton, Norwalk, University of Wisconsin, Jefferson County and Evanston plans. (All levels.)

————, "Three Examples of Team Teaching in Action," *Nation's Schools 65*:62-65, 102, 104, 108, 110, May, 1960. ("School Plant Design," *Nation's Schools 65*:75-82, June, 1960.) Good resource article describing major projects in country, conditions necessary for programs and details about staff, salary, duties of personnel, facilities. (All levels.)

————; Hagstrom, Ellis A.; and Robinson, Wade M., "Team Teaching in Elementary School," *School Review 68*:71-84, 1960. Excellent account of very effectively organized teaching-team concept on elementary level with special reference scheduling, grouping, personnel, organizational patterns.

————, and Mitchell, D. P., "New Concepts Demand Changes in School Design," *Nation's Schools 65*:75-77, 80-82, June, 1960. Implications of team teaching for architectural design of buildings. (All levels.)

Bahner, John M., "Grouping Within a School," *Childhood Education 36*:354-356, April, 1960. Account of modification of grade level grouping to fit beliefs for grouping requiring team approach. (Elem.)

————, "In Grades 4-6," *Reading Instruction in Various Patterns of Grouping,* Conference on Reading, Chicago University, 1959, pp. 95-98. Grouping in reading instruction. (Elem.)

Barmack, Frank, "Cooperative Cumulation and Improvement of English Teaching," *High Points 28*:52-56, April, 1946. Exploring idea of "universalizing" best in teachers' talents, interests and skills. (Sec.)

Barrett, H. O., "Large Group Instruction," *Ontario Journal of Educational Research,* Dept. of Ed. Research, Ontario College of Education, University of Toronto, Canada, Vol. IV, No. 2, pp. 142-145, Spring, 1962. Methodology in instruction and class organization. (Sec.)

Battrick, Delmer H., "How Do Team Teaching and Other Staff Utilization Practices Fit into the Instructional Program of a Junior High School," *NASSP Bulletin 46*:13-15, October, 1962. Scheduling. (H.S.)

Baynham, Dorsey, "School of Future in Operation," *Phi Delta Kappa 42*:350-354,

May, 1961. Good composite of information on Ridgewood H.S. Project. Well-written and detailed enough to be helpful. (Sec.)

———, "Selected Staff Utilization Projects in California, Georgia, Colorado, Illinois, Michigan, New York," *NASSP Bulletin* 46:15-98, January, 1962. Detailed descriptions of specific program in a survey of work in six states. (All levels.)

Beasley, Kenneth Lowell, "An Investigation of the Effect of Team Teaching upon Achievement and Attitudes in U.S. History Classes," *Dissertation Abstract*, Vol. 23, No. 9, p. 3256, 1963. Northwest University, 234 pp., 1962. Study of achievement and attitudes as outgrowths of team approach and reasons for preference. (H.S.)

Becker, Harry A., "Team Teaching," *Instructor* 71:43-45, June, 1962. Explores concept and and discusses use of AV materials in programs. (All levels.)

Beggs, David W., "A Success Story of Small and Large Group Instruction: The Decatur-Lakeview Plan," *Overview* 3: No. 12, December, 1962. Summary of one adaptation of the Trump Plan; deals with the success and failures of flexible scheduling as it relates to team teaching. (Sec.)

———, *Decatur-Lakeview Plan: A Practical Application of the Trump Plan.* Englewood Cliffs, N.J.: Prentice-Hall, Inc., 1964. Detailed report of the Decatur-Lakeview Plan after three years of operation; points out problems and gives an account of how one school organized teaching teams and a flexible schedule and used multi-media aids in instruction. (Sec.)

———, and Buffie, Edward G., "The Pitfalls and Promise of Large Group Instruction," *American School Board Journal*, January, 1964. Treatment of large group instruction with some practical hints for team teachers. (All levels.)

———, and Olivero, James L., "A Place out of Space . . . the Independent Study Carrel . . . and a Variety of Studies in Lakeview High School, Decatur, Illinois," *NASSP Bulletin* 46:193-202, January, 1962. Discussion of study carrel construction and use; review of special Lakeview programs related to team teaching. (Jr.H.S.-H.S.)

———; Redlich, Velda M.; and Olivero, James L., "Lakeview High School Year-End Report, 1961-62," mimeographed, Decatur Public Schools, Illinois. Comparative analysis of factors which could be easily quantified—library circulation, grade analysis, test analysis, etc.—of the school after a year of team teaching. (Jr.H.S.-H.S.)

Blake, John A., "The Master Teacher—A New Type of Specialist," *American Association of University Professors Bulletin* 40:239-252, June, 1954. Theoretical discussion on ideas about the master teacher plan but no inclusion of its practical application. (All levels.)

Bloomenshine, Lee L., "San Diego Uses Teaching Team Approach in Staff Utilization," *NASSP Bulletin* 43:217-219, January, 1959. Brief general description of one team approach, objectives, staff personnel and duties and basic procedures used. (Jr. H.S.-H.S.)

———, "Team Teaching in San Diego," *NASSP Bulletin* 44:180-196, January, 1960. Purposes team organization, evaluation, reactions, subject areas, problems met in program. (Jr.H.S.-H.S.)

Bodine, Ivan; Hollister, E. M.; and Sackett, Harry, "A Contribution to Team Teaching," *NASSP Bulletin* 46: 111-117, April, 1962. Team teaching of "American Problems" course. (Sec.)

Bovinet, Wesley G., "Intern Program, Team Teaching, and Language Laboratory at Glenbrook H.S.," *NASSP Bulletin* 43:249-254, January, 1959. Overview of six projects using team approach along with other techniques in different subject areas. (H.S.)

Braun, R. H., "Urbana, Ill. Sr. H.S. Changes Staff Patterns and Priorities for Superior Students," *NASSP Bulletin* 45:209-215, January, 1961. English team teaching project. (Sec.)

Brown, Charles I., "Make It a Team-Teaching Venture," *The Clearing House* 37:340-342, February, 1963. Teacher training teams (student and critic teacher as team). (Higher educ.)

Brownell, John A., and Taylor, Harris A., "Theoretical Perspectives for Teaching Teams," *Phi Delta Kappan* 43:150-157, January, 1962. Defines team members and describes operational procedures. (All levels.)

Bush, R. N., "Editorial! The Team Teaching Bandwagon," *California Journal of Secondary Education* 35:207-208, April, 1960. Cautioning "too quick" jump on team teaching "bandwagon" will merit close study. (Sec.)

————, "Searching Appraisal of New Developments," *California Journal of Secondary Education* 37:321-326, October, 1962. Editorial comments on team teaching and flexible group. (Sec.)

Cahall, T. Wilson, "Team Teaching in the Elementary School," *Grade Teacher* 78:62, 117, 122, November, 1960. Some advantages of division of staff labor and utilization of staff specialities and specialists. (Elem.)

Cashen, Valjeanor, "Using Specialists as a Team," *Educational Leadership* 19: 115-117, November, 1961. Meaning and role of "specialist." (Sec.)

Clark, Arvel B., "Administering Team Teaching in East Side District, San Jose, Calif.," *NASSP Bulletin* 46:141-144, January, 1962. Facilities, supervision and public relations. (Sec.)

Clawson, H. A., "English and Science Studies in Mattoon Sr. H.S.," *NASSP Bulletin* 44:257-263, January, 1960. Description of English and science orientation to team approach. (Sec.)

————, "Science Lecture and Team Approaches in English Are Tried in Mattoon H.S.," *NASSP Bulletin* 43:245-247, January, 1959. Science and English experimental techniques in grouping and purposes of approach. (H.S.)

Clement, Stanley L., "More Time for Teaching," *NASSP Bulletin* 46:54-59, December, 1962. How to utilize team techniques in order to employ teaching talents more wisely. (All levels.)

Congreve, Willard J., "Toward Independent Learning," *North Central Association Quarterly*, Vol. XXXVII, No. 4, pp. 298-302, Spring, 1963. Flexible programming, teaching techniques, scheduling. (Sec.)

Conner, Berenice G., "Let Your Enthusiasm Show," *English Journal* 50:626-628, December, 1961. English literature team teaching project. (Sec.)

Cooper, Walter L., "Use of Tapes, Language Lab, and Teaching Teams of J. Sterling Morton H.S. and Jr. College," *NASSP Bulletin* 44:233-243, January, 1960. Description of team approach to teaching American history and American literature. (H.S.-Jr. Coll.)

Cope, Mrs. Charles W., and Medley, William, "Winfield, Kansas, H.S. Pioneers Team Teaching," *NASSP Bulletin* 46:167-172, January, 1962. Problems and merits of teaching team through voices of those associated with it. (Sec.)

Cordry, Vernon, "A More Flexible Schedule at Fremont," *California Journal of Secondary Education* 35:114-116, February, 1960. Team teaching project in Social Studies (scheduling). (Sec.)

Cunningham, Luvern L., "Keys to Team Teaching," *Overview* 1:54-55, October, 1960. Administrative problems in team teaching. (Sec.)

————, "Team Teaching: Where Do We Stand?" *Administrator's Notebook* 8:1-4, April, 1960. Describes four team types, aimed toward appeal to administrators. (All levels.)

Dean, Ray B., "Team Teaching in Elementary Schools," *American School Board Journal*, 145:5-6, December, 1962. Organizational patterns of team approach—combines departmentalized and self-contained plan. (Elem.)

Dean, Stuart E., "Team Teaching: A Review," *School Life* 44:5-8, September, 1961. A general review of ideas regarding team teaching.

Dillow, Carl L., "Taylorville, Ill. Sr. H.S. Uses Tape Recorders, Team Teaching, and Large Group Instruction to Improve Staff Utilization," *NASSP Bulletin* 45:178-188, January, 1961. Large group approach to team teaching. (Sec.)

Douglass, H. R., *Modern Administration of Secondary Schools*. Boston: Ginn & Co., 1963, pp. 90-92, 383-385. Staff organization and scheduling in reference to Trump-type plan. (H.S.)

Downey, Lawrence W., "Direction Aimed Change," *Phi Delta Kappan* 42:186-191, February, 1961. Guidelines for educational change(s). (All levels.)

Drummond, Harold D., "Team Teaching: An Assessment," *Educational Leadership* 19:160-165, December, 1961. Overview of significant types, advantages, arguments against certain approaches. (All levels.)

Durrell, Donald O., "Implementing and Evaluating Pupil-Team Learning Plans," *Journal of Educational Sociology* 34:360-365, April, 1961. Specifically concerned with Dedham "team-learning plan." (All levels.)

————, "Team Learning," *Grade Teacher* 77:20, 87, 88, June, 1960. Description of "working" and structure of team learning plan. (Elem.)

Eakin, Gladys A., and Spence, Eugene S., "Team Teaching and Independent Reading," *Elementary English*, Vol. XXIX, No. 3, pp. 266-268, March, 1962. Basis for grouping content of program scheduling, working with slow readers. (Elem.)

Elliott, Richard W., "Team Teaching: Effective In-Service Training," *American School Board Journal* 144:19, February, 1962. Team teaching as in-service training. (All levels.)

Evans, Harley, "Stirrings in Big Cities: Cleveland," *NEA Journal* 51:50-53, November, 1962. Cleveland team project. (Elem.)

Fischler, Abraham S., "The Use of Team Teaching in the Elementary School," *School Science and Math* 62:287-288, April, 1962. Presents theoretical model for TT elementary school and illustrates major difficulties inherent in its structure. (Elem.)

———, and Shoresman, Peter B., "Team Teaching in Elementary School: Implications for Research in Science Instruction and Education," *Science Education* 46:405-415, December, 1962. Team teaching models and problems for research. (Elem.)

Ford, Paul M., "A Different Day for the English Teacher," *English Journal* 50: 334-337, May, 1961. Team approach in English instruction. (Sec.)

Formsma, Jay W., "A New High School with a New Look," *North Central Association Quarterly*, Vol. XXXVII, No. 4, pp. 293-297, Spring, 1963. Changes in facilities, scheduling, curriculum. (Sec.)

Gambold, Willard J., "The Modern Teacher and New Media of Instruction," *Education* 83:67-70, October, 1962. Discussion of team teaching as a new "media" in methodology and curriculum development. (All levels.)

Gilchrist, Robert S., "Promising Practices in Education, II," *Phi Delta Kappan* 41:27, March, 1960. Mentions Norwalk and Evanston plans and the three goals of team teaching that are presently being tested. (All levels.)

Ginther, John R., and Shroyer, William A., "Team Teaching in English and History at Eleventh Grade Level," *School Review* 90:303-313, Autumn, 1962. Summary of research findings on team approach in English and history. (Sec.)

Glancy, Philip B., "Brookside Jr. Hi., Sarasota, Florida, Strives for Quality Education," *NASSP Bulletin* 46:157-162, January, 1962. Experiment in team approach—flexibility, organization, facilities, purposes and strengths. (Jr.H.S.)

Gordon, Ira J., "Determining Teacher Effectiveness," *Educational Leadership*, 119-125, November, 1962. Related research in teacher effectiveness. (All levels.)

Grieder, Calvin, "The Administrator's Clinic," *Nation's Schools* 70:10, 20, October, 1962. Subsection: "Team Teaching: Just Another Kick?" Problems involved in its execution. (All levels.)

Gross, Calvin E., "Team Teaching in Pittsburgh," *Education Digest* 28:12-15, November, 1962. Report of Pittsburgh's large team project—types of patterns on all levels, members, few strengths are noted. (All levels.)

Gross, R. E., "Emerging Horizons for Social Studies, *Social Education* 24:21-24, January, 1960. Team approach in social studies. (Sec.)

Haeckel, Lester C., "Facilities for Elementary Team Teaching," *American School Board Journal* 146:27-28, January, 1963. Facilities for teaching teams. (Elem.)

Hagstrom, Ellis A., "New Opportunity for Outsanding Teachers," *Grade Teacher* 78:13, 104, January, 1961, (Elem.)

Hahn, Robert; Nelson, Jack; and Robinson, Gertrude, "Team Teaching: A Second Look," *Journal of Teacher Education* 12:508-510, December, 1961. Evaluation attempt in teacher education by team approach. (Sec.)

Harrison, William J., "Team Teaching at Muskegon, Michigan, Sr. H.S.," *NASSP Bulletin* 46:239-242, January, 1962. The uniqueness and flexibility of program are justified in this general description. (H.S.)

Harvey, Robert, and Tenenberg, Morton S., "University of Chicago Lab School, Illinois, Evaluates Team Teaching," *NASSP Bulletin* 45:189-197, January, 1961. "Facilitator" and "composition" of groups. (Sec.)

Hathaway, Larry, "Team Teaching in Illinois H.S.," *American Teacher* 46:11-12, 22, April, 1962. Teaching team project in Illinois. Looks closely at teacher, student and "essentials of program. (Sec.)

Heller, Melvin P., "Teamwork in Curriculum Planning," *Illinois Education*, Vol. 51, No. 5, pp. 195-196, January, 1963. Comprehensive article dealing with in-service training regarding curriculum planning, materials, evaluation, and administrative organization, supervising and evaluation. (H.S.)

———, and Belford, Elizabeth, "Team Teaching and Staff Utilization in Ridgewood H.S.," *NASSP Bulletin* 46:105-122, January, 1962. General discussion of specific aspects of team program involving teachers, administrators and students. (Sec.)

————, and Belford, Elizabeth, "Hierarchy in Team Teaching," *NASSP Bulletin* 46:59-64, December, 1962. Discussion of status, leadership, authority and duties of team members. (Sec.)

Hemeyer, Will, and McGrew, Jean B., "Big Ideas for Big Classes," *School Review* 68:308-317, Autumn, 1960. Associate teaching project in social studies. (Sec.)

Hoopes, Ned F., "The Training Process for Team Teaching," *Journal of Teacher Education* 14:177-178, June, 1963. Teacher training for team teaching. (All levels.)

Hoppock, Anne, "Team Teaching: Form without Substance," *NEA Journal* 50:47-48, April, 1961. Discusses the types of improvements TT should produce and how quality of this teaching differs from conventional method. (All levels.)

Howe, Harold, "The Curriculum, the Team, and the School: An Examination of Relationships," *California Journal of Secondary Education* 37:353-361, October, 1962. (All levels.)

Hurley, Wm.; Ceresa, Aldo; Songer, Ada; Pacoti, Louise; Clawson, Aileen; and Chrisman, Byron, "Team Teaching and Use of Recorders in Taylorville Sr. H.S.," *NASSP Bulletin* 44:268-274, January, 1960. Team approach in English. (Sec.)

Hyer, A. L. (Ed.); DuBois, L. D.; and Kain, A., "We Find the Walls Get in the Way (An Interview)," *Audio-Visual Instructor* 7:528-533, October, 1962. Excellent article on detailed suggestions for construction and use of space and facilities in Jr.H.S. situation. (Jr.H.S.)

Jensen, Lawrell; Riggle, Wanda B.; Merkley, Philip; Nielson, Virginia; and Rudy, Rhoda, "Eighth Grade Team Teaching at Roosevelt Jr. High School," *California Journal of Secondary Education* 35:236-243, April, 1960. Team teaching experiment on better utilization of time and competence of teachers. (Jr. H.S.)

Johnson, Robert H., and Lobb, M. Delbert, "Jefferson County, Colorado, Completes Three Year Study of Staffing, Changing Class Size, Programming and Scheduling," *NASSP Bulletin* 45:57-78, January, 1961.

————, "The Transformation of Sacred Secondary-School Schedule," *California Journal of Secondary Education* 35:96-105, February, 1960. Team teaching and schedule modification project. (Sec.)

————; Lobb, M. D.; and Patterson, Gordon, "Continued Study of Class Size, Team Teaching and Scheduling in Eight High Schools in Jefferson City, Colorado." *Bulletin of NASSP* 243:99-103, January, 1959. Discussion mostly concerning class size and scheduling and staff personnel. (Sec.)

————; Lobb, M. Delbert; and Swenson, Lloyd G., "An Extensive Study of Team Teaching and Modification of Schedule in Jefferson County, Colo. School District R-1," *NASSP Bulletin* 44:78-93, January, 1960. Basic research in team teaching concepts and schedule changes—organization patterns. (H.S.)

Jonsson, Stewart R., "Team Teaching? Enthusiasm Is High," *N.Y. State Education*, pp. 14-17, November, 1962. Project in team teaching in math, biology, and world history and English. (H.S.)

King, Arthur R., Jr., "Planning for Team Teaching, The Human Considerations," *California Journal of Secondary Education* 37:362-367, October, 1962. Discusses nature of operating school using team method and teaching team impact on human factors in process. (All levels.)

Kivett, Ruth S., "Team Teaching Is Tops," *Indiana Teacher* 106:368-370, May, 1962. Team teaching in biological science, math, English, history and chemistry. (Sec.)

Lalime, Arthur W., "Elementary Schools Designed for Team Teaching," *Audio-Visual Instructor* 7:540-541, October, 1962. Characteristics of teaching teams and building specification as well as details on AV materials (possibly used by us). (Elem.)

Lambert, Philip, "Team Teaching for the Elementary School," *Education Digest*, Vol. XXVI, No. 6, pp. 5-7, February, 1961. Pros of TT as seen through practical class situations, advantages and problems involved in its initiation. (Elem.)

————, "Team Teaching for the Elementary School," *Educational Leadership* 18:85-89, 128, November, 1960. Classroom situations illustrating advantages of team effort—plus problems and further claims for it. (Elem.)

————, "Team Teaching for Today's World," *Teachers College Record* 64:480-486, March, 1963. Discusses theoretical elements relating to team approaches. (All levels.)

Lanning, Thomas E., and Weaver, Robert J., "Multiple Grouping and Teamwork," *Ohio Schools*, Vol. XL, No. 8, pp. 28-29, November, 1962. Science—integration of TT with regular classes. (Elem.)

Larmee, Roy A., and Ohm, Robert, "University of Chicago Lab School Freshman Project Involves Team Teaching, New Faculty Position, and Regrouping of Students," *NASSP Bulletin* 44:275-289, January, 1960. Teaching team approach, staff organization and regrouping techniques. (Sec.)

Lauder, Dick, "Team Teaching: Two Programs at Shoreline, Seattle High School," *College of Education Record*, University of Washington, Vol. XXIX, No. 3, pp. 29-38, March, 1963. Detailed description of scheduling, methodology, space, views, personnel and equipment given. (Sec.)

Lewis, Phyllis A., "Team Teaching—a Creative Approach," *Educational Horizons*, Vol. XLI, No. 1, pp. 11-14, Fall, 1962. Team approach plus community involvements aiding team teaching program. (Elem.)

Lonsdale, Bernard J., "Television and Team Teaching in California Elementary Schools," *California Journal of Elementary Education* 31:74-75, November, 1962. Includes bibliographic information and "sketches" of team teaching practices in different schools. (Elem.)

Loretan, Joseph O., "Team Teaching: Plus and Minus in New York's Junior High School," *NASSP Bulletin* 46:135-140, January, 1962. Experiment in flexible programming and large group teaching. (Jr.H.S.)

Marsh, Robert, "Team Teaching: New Concept?" *Clearing House* 35:496-499, April, 1961. (All levels.)

Menacker, Julius, "Inter-Departmental Team Teaching in H.S.," *Education Digest* 26:8-9, May, 1961. Possibilities for interdepartmental team effort and suggestions for implementation. (Sec.)

Michael, Lloyd, "Team Teaching," *NASSP Bulletin* 47:36-63, May, 1963. Definition of teaching team, various patterns, evaluation and brief account of examples of team effort. (Sec.)

Mitchell, Wanda B., "Why Try Team Teaching?" *NASSP Bulletin* 46:249-252, January, 1962. Some pros and cons of the team approach. (All levels.)

Morse, Arthur A., *Schools of Today—Tomorrow*. Garden City, N.Y.: Doubleday & Co., 1960. Report on educational experiments prepared for N.Y. State Education Department. (All levels.)

N. A., "A Critical Look at Team Teaching," *Instructor* 71:39-42, October, 1961. Discusses varying concepts, staffing, advantages, disadvantages, problems and many important aspects. (All levels.)

———, "Administrative Developments Discussion Groups," *NASSP Bulletin* 46:52-62, (53-54), October, 1962. Beginning procedures for team teaching suggested by J. Lloyd Trump and his proposals. (Sec.)

———, "An Administrator's Guide to Team Teaching," *Educational Executives' Overview*, Philadelphia: Buttenheim Publication, April, 1963, pp. 54-55. Administrative aid. (All levels.)

———, "An Experiment in Team Teaching," *NASSP Bulletin* 46:74-76, December, 1962. Some evaluation and limitations involved in a teaching team experiment. (Jr.H.S.)

———, "Some Opinions on Teacher Teams" (Transcription of a Discussion Among Staff Members). Laboratory School of University of Chicago, Illinois. February, 1961, 28 pp. Description of Chicago Laboratory teacher teams. (Elem.—Sec.)

———, "Summer Theme Stresses Technology Theme," *AV Instructor* 6:352-353, September, 1961. Types of programs—questions highlighting advantages of teaching teams. (All levels.)

———, "Symposium: Using Team Teaching to Individualize Instruction," *Journal of Secondary Education* 36:414-446, November, 1961. Series of discussions on many aspects of team teaching approach. (All levels.)

———, "Team Teaching: Specialists Combine to Instruct the Young," *Good Housekeeping* 153:144-145, October, 1961. Describes Lexington, Mass., elementary school program. (Elem.)

———, "Toward Improved School Organization," *National Elementary Principals* 41:115-127, December, 1961. Team teaching models of operation (simple and complex). (Elem.)

———, "What Is Happening in the Use of Teacher Teams and Teacher Assistants," *NASSP Bulletin* 46:326-328, April, 1961. Survey of activities within teaching team groups. (Sec.)

———, "What Responsibilities for the Principal in Organizing, Supervising, and Evaluating Teaching Teams," *NASSP Bulletin* 46:115-120, April, 1961.

Comments on administrative organization, evaluation and supervision of team teaching. (Sec.)

Nelson, Jack; Hahn, Robert O.; and Robinson, Gertrude A., "Team Teaching for Teacher Education: The New Approach," *Journal for Teacher Education 12*: 380-382, Semptember, 1961. Team teaching—project in teacher education. (Sec.)

Nelson, Roland H., ". . . And Here Is How an Educator Would Put the Perception Core into Effective Use," *Nation's Schools 65*:85-87, March, 1960. An architect's proposal in design and description to provide for elements of Trump's proposals. (Sec.)

Nesbitt, W. O., and Johnson, Palmer O., "Some Conclusions Drawn from the Snyder, Texas, Project," *NASSP Bulletin 44*:63-75, January, 1960. Teacher-team idea, aides, class size, material aids. (Jr.H.S.—H.S.)

Nichols, Aileen J., "Team Teaching," *Kentucky School Journal*, Vol. 41, No. 5, p. 20, January, 1963. Team teaching organization practices, methods, flexibility of space facilities, advantages. (Elem.)

Nimnicht, Glendon P., "A Second Look at Team Teaching," *NASSP Bulletin 46*:64-69, December, 1962. Discussion in some depth of basic assumptions in reference to team teaching, multi-class and large group instruction, and program design." (Sec.)

Noall, Matthew F., and Jensen, Lowell, "Team Teaching at Roosevelt Jr. H.S., Duchesne County, Utah," *NASSP Bulletin 44*:156-163, January, 1960. Student and teacher utilization, changes in curricular teaching design, reorganization of administrative patterns. (Jr.H.S.)

———, and Rose, Gale, "Team Teaching at Wahlquist Jr. H.S., Weber County, Utah," *NASSP Bulletin 44*:164-171, January, 1960. Description of experiment discussing organization, staff assignments, scheduling, evaluation and materials. (Jr.H.S.)

Norton, Monte S., "Approaches to Team Teaching," *NASSP Bulletin 44*:89-92, October, 1960. Description of different team approaches. (Jr.H.S.)

Pannwitt, Barbara S., "Evanston, Ill. Township H.S. Reports on Five Years of Projects, Including TV, Team Teaching, and Large and Small Group Instruction," *NASSP Bulletin 45*:244-248, January, 1961. Team teaching approach and grouping procedure for instruction. (Sec.)

Partridge, Arthur R., "Staff Utilization in Sr. H.S.," *Educational Leadership 18*:217-221, January, 1961. (Sec.)

Paullin, Charlene, "Team Teaching in General Music Classes in San Diego, Calif." *NASSP Bulletin 46*:203-208, January, 1962. Team approach used in the teaching of general music in Jr. H.S. (Sec.)

Perkins, Bryce, et al., "Teamwork Produces Audio-Visual Techniques," *Grade Teacher 77*:55-72, June, 1960. Excellent utilization of AV techniques and equipment in team teaching. (Elem.)

Perkins, Hugh V., "Non-Graded Programs, What Progress?" *Educational Leadership 19*:166-169, 194, December, 1961. Discussion of the "non-graded" idea in relation to school organization, and some of its characteristics. (All levels.)

Peterson, Carl H., "Is Team Teaching for Your Schools?" *American School Board Journal 145*:11-13, October, 1962. Values and limitations inherent in team teaching and large group instruction. (Sec.)

Pitruzzello, Philip R., "A Report on Team Teaching," *Clearing House 36*:333-336, February, 1962. Report on team instruction in six states and implications for research. (Sec.)

Ploghoff, Minton E., "Another Look at Team Teaching," *Clearing House 36*:219-221, December, 1961. Introspection into some "unspoken" propositions of team approaches. (All levels.)

Polos, Nicholas C., "Progress in Teacher Education—The Claremont Plan," *Journal of Teacher Education 11*:398-401, September, 1960. In-service "team" training and leadership seminar. (All levels.)

Rehage, R. J., "On Summer School Circuit," *Elementary School Journal 61*:1-3, October, 1960. Brief description of Madison, Wisconsin, project on all elementary grade levels. (Elem.)

Shumsky, Abraham, and Mukerji, Rose, "From Research Idea to Classroom Practice," *Elementary School Journal 63*:83-86, November, 1962. Applying theory to practice—stage of "implementation." (Elem.)

Singer, Ira S., "Survey of Staff Utilization Practices in Six States," *NASSP Bulletin 46*:1-13, January, 1962. Definitions of team teaching and chart showing various current practices in six states and summary. (Sec.)

Slichenmyer, H. L., "Arlington Hts., Ill., Studies Curriculum and Testing, Instruction Assistants, Team Teaching, and Modern Technology in Fourteen Projects," *NASSP Bulletin* 45:41-49, January, 1961. Team concept explored in different concepts within academic project areas. (Sec.)

Smith, Gjertrud, "Verdugo Hills, H.S., Tujunga, Calif., Introduces Split-Week Courses and Team Teaching to Add Flexibility to the Program," *NASSP Bulletin* 46:173-184, January, 1962. New scheduling techniques in a variety of subjects. (H.S.)

Smith, Verna, "Team Teaching in Geometry," *School and Community* 48:13, 28, April, 1962. Ritenow High School. General description of a team teaching attempt in math area—no specifics mentioned. (H.S.)

Smith, Vernon H., "Team Teaching Has Advantages," *English Journal* 49:242-244, April, 1960. Advantages of team teaching of English classes. (Sec.)

Stafford, Curt, "Teacher Time Utilization with Teacher Aides," *Journal of Educational Research*, Vol. 56, No. 2, pp. 82-88, October, 1962. Use of teacher aides in classroom—listing of daily tasks, observed on basis of a job analysis time study. (Elem.)

Stetson, G. Arthur, and Harrison, James P., "Junior High School Designed for Team Teaching," *American School Board Journal* 140:38-42, May, 1960. Facilities (floor play and equipment) for "horizontal type" concept teaching. (Jr.H.S.)

Stevens, John M., and Richards, A. Winston, "Team Teaching in World Geography—Jr. H.S.," *California Journal of Secondary Education* 35:244-245, April, 1960. Social studies experiment presented in limited manner but good pointers for different materials and techniques, plus more advantages felt. (Jr. H.S.)

Stoltenberg, James C., "Team Teaching in Junior H.S.," *Educational Leadership* 18:153-155, December, 1960. Experiment in unified English—social studies team approach. (Jr.H.S.)

Stone, W. J., "New Designs for Secondary School Scheduling," *California Journal of Secondary Education* 35:126-130, February, 1960. Scheduling objectives. (Jr.H.S.)

———, and Ramstad, Wm. K., "Team Teaching—The Results of a California Study," *California Journal of Secondary Education* 36:273-276, May, 1961. Reports from team teaching practices in six states. (Sec.)

Sweet, Raymond, and Dunn-Rankin, Peter, "An Experiment in Team Teaching Seventh Grade Arithmetic," *School Science and Math* 62:341-344, May, 1962. Experiment in team effort in area of math. (Jr.H.S.)

Szabb, Lester J., "Team Teaching: Honors Students Undergo Experiment," *New York State Education*, pp. 12-13, October, 1961. Especially helpful to social studies personnel on materials, types of methods, weaknesses needing attention in planning. (H.S.)

Taylor, Donald N., "A Study of Opinions of Educators Concerning Proposals to Reorganize Secondary Schools to Accommodate Large and Small Group Instruction, Independent Study, and Team Teaching," *Dissertation Abstract*, Vol. 23, No. 11, p. 4270, 1963. 175 pp., Columbia University, 1962. Opinions of educators and administrators regarding some of Trump's proposals in 1959. (Sec.)

Tenenberg, Morton S., *University of Chicago Laboratory School Freshman Staff Utilization Project Final Report, 1959-60*. 29 pp + appendix. Describe Chicago Laboratory teams in math, science and social studies. (Sec.)

Tracy, Edward, and Peterson, Carl H., "The Easton, Penn., Team Teaching Program," *NASSP Bulletin* 46:145-155, January, 1962. Detailed description of curricular program utilizing team teaching, highlighting flexible instruction, relationship of subject matter to pupil ability, motivational techniques, plans for new H.S. geared for special program. (H.S.)

Trump, J. Lloyd, "Flexible Scheduling: Fad or Fundamental," *Phi Delta Kappan* 44:367-371, May, 1963. Flexible scheduling. (Sec.)

———, "Images of the Future: A New Approach to Secondary Education," Urbana Commission on Experimental Study of the Utilization of Staff in Secondary School, *NASSP Bulletin*, January, 1959. Instructional staff. (Sec.)

———; Tillenwater, Virgil W.; and Rowhey, Charles D., "Summer Workshops on Staff Utilization," *NASSP Bulletin* 44:316-332, January, 1960. Summer workshop planning and recommendations for team teaching. (Sec.)

Varner, Glenn F., "Team Teaching in Johnson H.S. St. Paul, Minn.", *NASSP Bulletin* 46:161-166, January, 1962. Describes the reaction of staff, pupils and administrators as well as their challenge in implementing a team approach. (H.S.)

Walker, Wally, "Team Teaching: Pros and Cons," *CTA Journal* 58:17, April, 1962. AV equipment used by competent teachers which has been successful in large group instruction. (Sec.)

Ward, J. O., "Another Plan to Coordinate Teaching." *American School Board Journal* 140:10, February, 1960. Pros and Cons for coordinate teaching. (Elem.)

Watson, N. E., "Glenbrook H.S., Northbrook, Ill., Projects on Internship, Large Classes, Team Teaching, Teacher Aides, and Language Lab," *NASSP Bulletin* 45:51-56, January, 1961. Discussion of such activities as team teaching, class sizes, use of teaching aides. (Sec.)

Welchinger, C. T., "Promising Experimental Practices at Mainland Sr. H.S., Daytona Beach, Florida." (Presentation to one of the discussion groups at the Convention of the NASSP, held at Pittsburgh, Pa.) Describes three team teaching practices. (H.S.)

White, Robert William, "Relative Effectiveness of Team Teaching Methods in High School Biology Instruction," *Dissertation Abstract*, Vol. 23, No. 11, p. 4271, 1963, University of Wisconsin, 318 pp. (H.S.)

Woolbridge, James H., and Mayer, Frank E., "Building for Team Teaching," *Ohio Schools*, Vol. XL. No. 5, p. 15, May, 1962. Administrative organization. (All levels.)

Wynn, D. Richard, and DeRemer, Richard W., "Staff Utilization, Development, and Evaluation," *Review of Educational Research* 31:393-396, October, 1961. Research on staff use, development and evaluation as it is related to administration at local level. (All levels.)

TEAM TEACHING SCHOOLS

WHILE there have been many significant team teaching projects going on across the country, the following are listed as outstanding, yet representative examples:

Elementary Schools (x-6)

Baltimore Public Schools, Baltimore, Maryland
Barrington Elementary Schools, Barrington, Illinois
Elementary Schools, Mt. Diablo School District, Concord, California
Freedom Union School District, Oceano, California
Glen Ellyn Public Schools, Glen Ellyn, Illinois
Janesville Public Schools, Janesville, Wisconsin
Lechner Elementary School, Berea, Ohio
Lexington Public Schools, Lexington, Massachusetts (SUPRAD)
Lincoln Elementary School, Cedar Falls, Iowa
Maple Road Elementary School, Williamsville, New York
Moreland Elementary School, Shaker Heights, Ohio
Norwalk Public Schools, Norwalk, Connecticut (The Norwalk Plan)
Skyland Elementary Schools, DeKalb, Georgia

Junior High Schools (Grades 7-9)

Alfred Plant Junior High School, West Hartford, Connecticut
Brookside Junior High School, Sarasota, Florida
Fox Lane School, Bedford, New York
Lakeview Junior High School, Decatur, Illinois
Muzzey Junior High School, Lexington, Massachusetts
Newton Junior High Schools, Newton, Massachusetts
O'Farrell Junior High School, San Diego, California
Roosevelt Junior High School, Duchesne County, Utah (Salt Lake City)
University Junior High School, Indiana University, Bloomington, Indiana
Wahlquist Junior High School, Weber County, Utah
William T. Gordon Junior High School, Coatesville, Pennsylvania
Williamsville Junior High School, Williamsville, New York

Senior High Schools (10-12)

Amherst Central High School, Buffalo, New York
Brecksville High School, Brecksville, Ohio
East Irondoquoit High School, Rochester, New York
El Dorado High School, El Dorado, Arkansas
Freemont High School, Sunnydale, California
Holland High School, Holland, Michigan
Jefferson County Schools, Lakewood, Colorado
Lakeview High School, Decatur, Illinois
Newton High Schools, Newton, Massachusetts
Penn High School, Mishawaka, Indiana
Rich Township High School, Park Forest, Illinois
Ridgewood High School, Norridge, Illinois
San Diego Public Schools, San Diego, California
Solon High School, Solon, Ohio
S. P. Waltrip High School, Houston, Texas
Williamsville Central High School, Williamsville, New York

Index

A

accreditation agencies, 135
achievement tests, 114, 115-117
ad hoc scheduling, 39, 42, 67, 70
administrator, role of, 92-97, 120-123, 131-144
Advanced Placement Conferences, 140
Allen, Dr. Dwight W., 80, 136
Anaheim, Calif., 70-71, 79
"And No Bells Ring," 16
assumptions, of current teaching practices, 83-84; of team teaching, 47-48
attitude scales, 114-115

B

back-to-back scheduling, 67
Barrington Elementary Schools (Barrington, Ill.), 60
Barrington, Ill., 60
Bay City Teacher Aide Project, 24
Becker, Dr. Harry A., 160
block-of-time scheduling, 67
Bloomington, Ind., 67, 69
Brickell, Henry M., 28, 96
Brookhurst Junior High School (Anaheim, Calif.), 22, 79
"Brookhurst Plan, The," 80
Brown, B. Frank, 84
Bulletin of the National Association of Secondary School Principals, The, 16, 113, 130
Bush, Dr. Robert N., 80, 136

C

Carnegie Unit, 91
Carson City Elementary Schools (Carson City, Mich.), 60
Carson City, Mich., 60
cause and effect, 123-124
Chagrin Falls, Ohio, 60
Chagrin Falls Public Schools (Chagrin Falls, Ohio), 60

changes in elementary schools, 57-60
Claremont, Calif., 21
Claremont College (Claremont, Calif.), 16, 21
climate for change, 94-95
Commission on Curriculum Planning and Development, 15
Commission on the Experimental Study of the Utilization of Staff in the Secondary School, 84
Committee on Staff Utilization, 14, 16
Conant, James B., 124, 160
consultants, role of, 99
content, in team teaching, 35-36, 39, 155-163
Cooper, Gordon, 155
cooperation, 127, 151-152
core program, 72
creativity, 148-149
current teaching practices, 14-15

D

Decatur, Ill., 22, 47, 70, 102, 109, 147
Decatur-Lakeview Plan, 70
Deerfield, Mass., 60
Deerfield Elementary Schools (Deerfield, Mass.), 60
differentiated role specialist, 42, 43
"division," the, 20

E

Educational Facilities Laboratory (N. Y.), 135
El Dorado, Ark., 102
El Dorado Plan, 102
El Dorado Public Schools (El Dorado, Ark.), 102
Encyclopaedia Britannica School (Chicago), 88
evaluation (assessment) of team teaching, 104-117
Evanston, Ill., 21, 47, 70, 76, 109

189

Date Due

DEC 14 71			
OCT 30 74			
DEC 1 4 1983			
MAY 1 4 1984			
AUG 0 6 1986			
MAY 1 0 2000			